CW00919444

BAGA Women's Gymnastics Manual

BAGA Women's Gymnastics Manual

Colin Still, BAGA National Coach

SBL Springfield Books Limited

Copyright © 1990 Colin Still

Published by Springfield Books Limited,
Norman Road, Denby Dale, Huddersfield HD8 8TH,
West Yorkshire, England.

This book is copyright under the Berne Convention. All rights are
reserved. Apart from any fair dealing for the purposes of private
study, research, criticism or review, as permitted under the
Copyright Act, 1956, no part of this publication may be
reproduced, stored in a retrieval system, or transmitted in any form
or by any means, electronic, electrical, chemical, mechanical,
optical, photocopying, recording or otherwise, without the prior
written permission of the copyright owner. Enquiries should be
addressed to the publishers.

First edition 1990

Design: Douglas Martin
Illustrations: Meg Warren
Photography: Eileen Langsley, Supersport
Typesetting: BP Integraphics
Printed and bound in England by
Butler & Tanner, Frome, Somerset

British Library Cataloguing in Publication Data
Still, Colin
BAGA women's gymnastics manual: the official manual of
the British Amateur Gymnastics Association.
1. Women's gymnastics. Coaching
I. Title
796.44

ISBN 0–947655–28–X

jacket photo: Svetlana Boginskaya, USSR

frontispiece: Natalia Lashonova, USSR

To my wife Christine
and children Danielle and Hayley

Foreword

This book is one of the best researched, most carefully organised and thoughtfully structured books on women's gymnastics. The author, a well-respected 'hands-on' coach, has great experience at club, regional, national and international levels of gymnastics. While he was Chief Coach at Loughton Hall Gym Club, he and his wife produced Senior and Junior Championship teams for Great Britain and a string of good international gymnasts who competed at Olympic, World and European Championships (Senior and Junior), Gymnasiads and Universiads. His international experience – Team Coach for Great Britain since 1978 – has given him the opportunity to study our sport in many countries and to work with and discuss his subject with many of the best coaches in the world. He has led British teams to international training camps in the USA and USSR.

The selection of skills covered in this book is extremely pertinent to the development of a gymnast, and the book will be an invaluable aid in supporting the BAGA's coaching programme as well as giving good direction to already established coaches.

John Atkinson, MBE, FBISC
Technical Director, BAGA
Chairman, BISC

Contents

Acknowledgements

I should like to thank all of the following people for their contribution to this book. They are all experts in their field and the critical feedback I have received from them has been of inestimable assistance: John Atkinson, BAGA Technical Director; John Aldridge, Coventry and Warwick Hospital; John Brewer, FA Physiological Testing Centre; Jackie Cross, Tesco Foods Ltd; Lew Hardy, University College of North Wales, Bangor; Mike Haynes, Trafford School of Gymnastics; Hazel Malpass, BAGA Brevet Judge; John Newton, Carnegie Department, Leeds Polytechnic; Pauline Newton, FA National Rehabilitation Centre; Lyn Pateman, Coventry and Warwick Hospital; Graham Smith, Glasgow Rangers Football Club; Karen Sprunt, Carnegie Department, Leeds Polytechnic; and Carole White, Rowley Park Hospital. I am especially indebted to Hazel Wearmouth, who contributed the chapter on 'The prudent coach: legal considerations'. She is a Senior Lecturer at the Carnegie Department, Leeds Polytechnic, working in the areas of philosophy, legal liability and gymnastics. In the sport of recreational gymnastics she chairs the Yorkshire and Humberside Regional Technical Committee and the National Technical Committee, and she is also vice-president of the General Gymnastics Technical Commission of the Union of European Gymnastics. I am most grateful to her for dealing with this area within the book.

Colin Still
BAGA National Coach (Women's Teams)

Introduction

The aim of this book is to help teachers and coaches reach a clear understanding of the steps involved in producing a good gymnast. Part I covers the basic theory you will need in order to appreciate the skills detailed in Part II, so it would be sensible to read this first. In Part II, core gymnastics elements have been selected and described, and the necessary techniques explained. In addition, these movements have been subjected to mechanical analysis, and the progressions required for their ultimate success have been tabulated. The range of movement entailed, specific conditioning and any other prerequisites are indicated.

The results presented here are a distillation of my years of experience in the sport of gymnastics, supported by the scientific knowledge of Karen Sprunt from Leeds Polytechnic. They are intended to provide a clear impression of the magnitude and direction of the forces involved in each skill analysed.

The progressions needed to achieve a move are many and varied. I have used those which I personally have found most successful. However, I would emphasise that it should always be remembered that each individual gymnast is different, and we must continue to search for new progressions. Never accelerate the learning process. Remember that the teacher or coach is responsible for ensuring that the gymnast's motivation always stays high, and her anxiety level low.

Part I
Theoretical background

1 Planning the training

The teacher or coach, and sometimes the mature gymnast, is responsible for the construction of routines, selecting skills and the competition programme. If insufficient thought goes into this work, then the gymnast may not maximise her potential. It is very important that time is taken to structure the work so that the desired progress is made each year. Both long-term and short-term planning have to be taken into account.

Long-term planning

First you must assess the quality of the gymnast and what level she is likely to reach; has she the makings of an international, national, regional or a club gymnast? To do this you must look at her physical and psychological profiles. After assessing these, you must consider the possible improvements she could make, given certain factors. These include time, facility, coaching expertise, educational pressures, parental support, the age of the gymnast, and the effects any changes would have on the family unit as they affect the gymnast. You will then be in a position to programme most of the competitions up to four years ahead. Knowing the competition load each year, you can then decide which moves should be taught for which competitions. If the competition season is very heavy, then either less work can be done in that year or the gymnast must not enter some of the competitions.

In a four-year plan, the teacher or coach must decide which two competitions each year are going to be the 'peak' competitions. They should be roughly six months apart. The other competitions can then be highlighted as warm-up or developmental competitions. These projected routines, which can still be changed at any stage, will then set the structure for the yearly, monthly and weekly programmes.

Short-term planning

A one-year training plan can be considered as short-term. Within this time there are normally two competition periods. The competition to

Daniela Silivas, Romania

'peak' for should have already been decided in the long-term planning strategy. This type of planning is normally known as 'periodisation of training'.

One-year training programme

Element training	Pre-competition training	Competition period	Rest
Individual elements	Combinations	Full routines	Active rest
Some combinations	Part routines	Specific conditioning	
General conditioning	General and specific conditioning		

Element training

All the elements that are going to make up the full routine will be taught to perfection and trained at this stage. A general conditioning programme needs to be done alongside this work, since the element training itself does not tax the gymnast enough, especially her local muscular endurance.

Pre-competition training

The time-span for pre-competition training may vary according to the number of hours in the gym, the general fitness of the gymnast, or how long she needs psychologically to settle into routines. Combinations of elements and part routines should be undertaken at this time. General conditioning and some specific conditioning should also continue. The gymnast is now beginning to become taxed during training because of the number of part routines, and the conditioning programme can be lighter. A little more time can now be spent on conditioning specific weak areas.

Competition period

Complete routines will be put together, trained and competed during this period. Some competitions should be treated as training competitions to gauge how fit the gymnast is for the 'peak' competition. Specific conditioning should be done at this stage. The routines being performed in the gym should now provide conditioning in themselves, and more time can be spent on any physically weak areas which need special attention.

Active rest period

After a long competition season the gymnast needs a physical and psychological rest from gymnastics. This period is set aside for her to take up another physical activity such as tennis or swimming, maintain muscle tone and generally unwind.

The short-term schedule

Before the schedule can be prepared, you will need to compile certain information:

1. The age of the gymnast
2. Weight
3. Height
4. Pubertal development
5. Ability
6. Skills and combinations to be taught
7. Does the gym have the equipment for the chosen skills?
8. How many sessions in the gym, and of what duration, will the gymnast train each week?
9. How much time is available to be worked on each apparatus each week?
10. Are there any areas of weakness in the gymnast's work that may require a bias towards a certain piece of apparatus?

A training schedule can now be put together which will eventually produce the required results. It is your responsibility to make sure that the gymnast keeps to the schedule. Since it is impossible to keep track of each gymnast's work all of the time, a record must be kept of the schedule and the success/failure rate of the work. This can be done in a diary or on the timetable that sets out the day's programme. At the end of the session the successes can be compared against the attempts. It is important to re-assess the programme and make changes when and where necessary. If an accurate record is kept, then when the gymnast is approaching a competition you can see the percentage of successes of elements and complete routines and decide whether to make changes or stay with the routine for that competition.

Other information to go into a training diary would be:

- Four-year plan, one-year plan, one-month plan, one-week plan
- Injuries
- Testing, e.g. strength increase, flexibility increase, standing height, sitting height, weight
- Chart of training intensity
- Competition results

Many coaches only pay lip service to planning the training. Initially it can be difficult and time-consuming. But if the time is spent correctly then both coach and gymnast feel happier and more motivated. Sometimes it is easier to programme a group of gymnasts of like ability in their early years and only individualize them at a later stage.

As teacher or coach, you need a strategy: when you should introduce physical pressures, when you should introduce psychological pressures. In the last week of training before a competition the physical work should have been done and can tail off to some extent. In a competition it is the psychological pressures that are more likely to affect the gymnast. These must be introduced to the gymnast in training. But how much, and of what intensity? These decisions need to be made, then the competition has to run its course before any changes are made in the build-up to the next competition. Such changes can only be made accurately with reference to the gymnast's past training schedule.

2 Training for strength

Basic principles

Gymnastics is very demanding upon the body and can only be enjoyed and mastered if the body is strong enough to accept the strain placed upon it. It is therefore essential to undertake the right preparation so as to accelerate skill learning and prevent injury.

There are certain basic principles which need to be understood.

1. Skeletal muscle is controlled by the central nervous system. Messages are sent from the brain via the central nervous system to the muscles to make them work.
2. Muscles are arranged in pairs. They are known as agonists and antagonists (sometimes protagonists). The partner muscles work in opposition to one another. As one contracts the other relaxes and vice-versa.
3. Muscular strength can be defined as the greatest amount of force that muscles can produce in a single maximal effort (see David R. Lamb, *Physiology of Exercise*, 1984).

The three major techniques available to strengthen the body are:

1. *Isotonic contraction.* A muscle contracts whilst changing length through part or all of a range of motion against a constant resistance, e.g. a chin to a bar.
2. *Isokinetic contraction.* The muscle contracts against a resistance which varies throughout the entire range of movement, dependent upon the force exerted. This is done using expensive electronic or hydraulic machines.
3. *Isometric contraction.* A muscle contracts and then does not change length, e.g. holding a chin position.

Isotonic and isokinetic contractions move through a range, as opposed to isometric contractions which are static. They can also be defined as concentric or eccentric, depending upon whether the muscle is shortening or lengthening. A chin-up would be an isometric concentric contraction, because the active muscles are shortening; whilst the reverse movement would be an isometric eccentric contraction, because the active muscles are lengthening.

Motor nerve efficiency

Training for strength is not solely dependent on increasing muscle size. Through the motor nerves, the brain sends electrical messages to the muscles to fire and make contractions. The number of motor units recruited depends upon the force of contraction required. It seems possible through training to recruit more units and fire them simultaneously and therefore make larger contractions resulting in greater strength.

Strength is dependent on the size of the muscle and on these neural pathways. It is possible for someone to become stronger after exercise because of a more efficient recruitment of motor nerves rather than through an increase in the cross-sectional area of the muscle.

The 'overload principle'

Teacher and coach must appreciate that the human organism will specifically adapt to an imposed demand. Therefore if the demand on the muscles is progressively increased there will be an improvement in strength.

Whether the gymnast wishes to improve strength, power or endurance, she must work in the 'fatigue zone'. The principle underlying this technique is called the 'overload principle'. First, a load has to be applied to the body. The body will initially experience fatigue and then recover. But instead of returning to its original starting point it super-compensates to a new performance level.

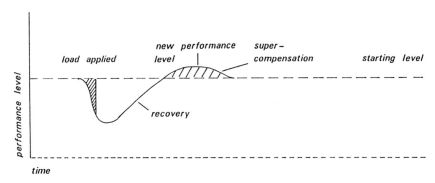

The load adaptation curve

If this cycle is continued at regular intervals then new performance heights will be reached and the gymnast will become stronger and/or more powerful.

It is important to gauge when to increase the loading. If it is done too quickly, a downward spiral will occur and the gymnast will be continually exhausted. To increase strength the gymnast must train a specific muscle three to four times a week. To maintain the gain in strength,

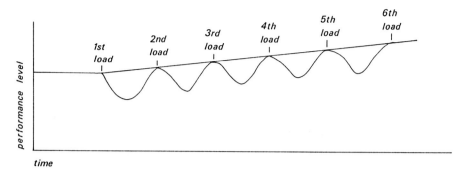

Regular interval loading to increase strength

the gymnast only needs to train twice a week. It is important to check and probably change the loading every two to three weeks. When the muscle has made its adaptation to a load, a heavier load is needed. The percentage of maximum load and the number of repetitions (reps) is selected according to the type of strength desired.

In the main, gymnasts use their own body weight as resistance. If this can be done whilst choosing exercises which relate closely to gymnastic skills, then this is highly desirable. To find the maximum load for the gymnast for any given exercise, first ask her to perform the exercise in its easiest form and then progressively make it more difficult until she can only do one repetition. Percentages can then be worked out. For example, the easiest form of press-up is performed standing upright against a wall. The most difficult form of press-up is done in a handstand position. Somewhere between these two extremes will be the maximum load for most gymnasts. It is best to use the number of reps the gymnast can achieve as the indicator of the type of strengthening it will achieve. For example, if a gymnast can only achieve five press-ups in any given position, then she will be conditioning for strength. If she could do fifty in that position, she would be conditioning for endurance.

There is some difference of opinion among exercise physiologists as to how the desired results may be achieved, but the following table will give you a basic guide to their findings.

	To increase max. strength	To increase power	To increase endurance
% max. load	80–95	50–80	25–50
No. of reps	6–8	15–25	30–50
No. of sets	3	3	2

Methods of strength training

Developing maximum strength

There are two widely used methods of developing maximum strength.

1. *Progressive resistance.* This technique is most favoured by gymnastics coaches as it lends itself very well to working the gymnast's body against gravity through the range of motion that is closely related to an element of gymnastics. This is highly desirable, so the technique should be followed whenever possible. A near-maximal load is used and the performer does about eight repetitions, repeated three times. It is important that a rest period of about five or six times the duration of the set is given between each set of repetitions. Another exercise, using different muscle groups, can be performed in this time. If the load is progressively increased over a period of time on the 'overload principle' already described, the maximum strength of the gymnast will gradually increase.

2. *Pyramid training.* This technique works well with fixed or free weights, but is not so accurate using the gymnast's body weight against gravity. Gymnasts have little skill in or experience of lifting free weights and should not be encouraged to do so. Fixed weights in a multi-gym are useful, but only under very strict supervision and with a high ratio of coaches to gymnasts.

   The gymnast should find the maximum load she can lift. She should then lift percentages of this weight as follows:

Set 1	70%	7 reps
Set 2	75%	6 reps
Set 3	80%	5 reps
Set 4	85%	4 reps
Set 5	90%	3 reps
Set 6	100%	1 rep

Developing speed and power

Once the gymnast has gained strength she can develop speed and power for certain dynamic aspects of her work such as running, jumping and flight off the hands. *Speed* is the ability of the neuromuscular system to produce the greatest possible impulse in the shortest possible time-span. Training for this should incorporate high-speed contractions with light resistance. *Power* is the ability of the neuromuscular system to continue developing the previously-initiated tension increase as rapidly as possible. Power = Force × Speed (or force × distance/time). To train for this, use 30–60% of the maximal force in high-speed contractions.

Plyometric training

This is really a sub-division of power and speed training. It is not advisable to use this method with pre-pubescent gymnasts, because the bones have not yet formed well enough. Osgood-Schlatters Disease of the knee and Severs Disease of the heel are all-too-common consequences of the use of this technique at too early a stage in the gymnast's development.

The technique involves pre-stretching a muscle prior to shortening it. It is estimated that about 30% more energy can be gained using this technique. The energy is stored because of the elastic qualities of muscles, myofibrils, cell tissues and tendons.

Examples of plyometrics would be rebound jumps or jumps from a height sufficient to result in immediate rebound response. To achieve this the gymnast should use a height that ensures that when she rebounds from the floor the heel of her foot does not touch the ground. This exercise should have 3–5 sets of ten repetitions, with a rest period between sets of about ten minutes. The principle does not only apply to the lower body; it can relate to any part of the body. Small rebound jumps off the hands would be just as effective, but again are not recommended for young gymnasts.

Endurance training

Endurance is the ability of the neuromuscular system to produce the ultimate performance in a defined time-span by resisting fatigue in long-term strength performances. Local muscular endurance is needed in the training gym for extended workouts when exercises need to be repeated many times. Initially it was thought that less than ten repetitions increased strength and more than ten repetitions increased endurance. It is now thought that more than ten reps (15–25) will still increase strength but will also increase short-term endurance. Higher numbers of reps with less weight are used to work towards intermediate endurance and finally long-term endurance.

The load for endurance exercises should be 30–50% of the maximum if the gymnast is training for medium endurance. The number of repetitions can be 30–50, with two sets being attempted.

Circuit training can also be very beneficial in improving endurance. Motivation stays high, different muscle groups can be worked one after the other, and the circuit can reflect gymnastic elements. An added bonus is an increase in cardiovascular endurance. The progressive overload can be achieved either by decreasing the rest period or by increasing the repetitions or the time spent on the exercise.

Very light weights can be used for some of the exercises, but generally the gymnast's own body weight against gravity will suffice. Inclining or declining the position of the body should change the load; if this is not sufficient then the coach can assist.

Variations in strength, age and gender

It should be remembered that no two gymnasts who are pre-pubescent and of the same age should be considered as having the same strength. Their strength develops with maturity and this progresses at different rates in different children. One child may have smaller muscles and a less highly developed nervous system than the other, and she will therefore not be as strong at that point in time. Only when maturation has taken place in both gymnasts can their strengths be compared, and this may well be at different chronological ages.

Most females, after strength training, do not develop the same amount of muscle bulk as their male counterparts due to the lower levels of testosterone in the body. Muscle definition is usually good in the female gymnast because of the lower levels of subcutaneous fat tissue that normally covers the body. The trained athlete's absolute strength is greatest between the ages of about twenty and thirty-five years. Before and after this the muscle mass is generally smaller, resulting in less strength.

Pre-pubescent gymnasts

Pre-pubescent children should be treated as a third species alongside men and women. They are different and should be treated as such. In the context of conditioning, the growing plates of the long bones must be protected against damage.

Because of the immaturity of their bodies, young gymnasts should not be lifting near-maximal weights. Training with free weights requires skill and should not be encouraged. Fixed weights are safer but restrictive; they do not allow the gymnast to simulate a gymnastic skill whilst conditioning. The best place to condition is in the gym.

Training times

For a gymnast to maximise the benefit from a strength programme she should condition when she is fresh. This will facilitate a stronger reaction from the muscles and neural pathways, resulting in a larger gain.

For gymnasts who train every other day this means that conditioning should be done on the rest days. For gymnasts who train most days, conditioning should be done at the beginning of each training session. A balance must be struck between the overall gains in strength and the necessary fatigue caused. You must remember that after conditioning, the gymnast will have to perform gymnastic skills which require a high degree of muscle co-ordination. A case could be made for not conditioning on days when high-level gymnastic skills are being performed. Alternatively, conditioning can be done at the end of training if it is accepted that the benefits will not be as great because body and mind are both tired. If two training sessions are possible in one day, then conditioning should be done at the beginning of the first session. The gap between the two training sessions should be as long as possible to allow for recovery and then the second training session can incorporate the more difficult gymnastic elements which may require the maximum response from the muscles.

The gymnast needs strength and power to perform certain elements within set routines. She also needs local muscular endurance in training to reproduce much of the work. The conditioning programme should reflect this. For a certain muscle to respond after a conditioning session, it will need a day's rest. For those gymnasts who train once a day every day, it might be better to condition a combination of upper body one day and lower body the next, or anterior muscles one day and posterior the next.

Designing a conditioning programme

All the following points need to be taken into consideration in designing a conditioning programme.

1. Every conditioning programme should be tailor-made for the individual gymnast. The overload principle must be used, causing the gymnast to experience fatigue.
2. The programme should not fatigue the gymnast to total exhaustion as this will affect the next day's training or require a longer recovery period.
3. Correct technique is very important. If possible it should simulate a gymnastic move but not be so difficult that good form is lost.
4. The gymnast should understand which muscle group is being exercised and how it needs to be isolated to have maximum effect.
5. Conditioning can be soul-destroying. The teacher or coach needs to motivate the gymnast for her to get good results. You need to explain the importance of conditioning, how it decreases anxiety, helps confidence and is essential for learning all gymnastic skills.
6. Try to design the programme so that it exercises different muscle groups in rotation.
7. Consideration must be given to the fitness level, experience, age, maturation level, and specific needs of each gymnast.
8. Test the effectiveness of the programme every two to three weeks.

3   Training for flexibility

Flexibility is of paramount importance to gymnasts. It enables them to perform their sport safely and with good technique, and to produce an aesthetically pleasing result.

The amount of flexibility any joint can have is governed by certain factors, such as the bone structure of the joint, cartilage tissue, the length of the ligaments and tendons and other connective tissue. The muscle bulk that has been developed is also a factor. Age, body type, the sort of day the gymnast has had, humidity can also affect the range of movement. The warmth of the body and surroundings has always been accepted as a factor, but recent research indicates that the time of day may also be a factor. However, since research is still being done in this area it would be prudent to continue with accepted practice until hard evidence suggests otherwise.

As already mentioned in relation to strength training, muscles contract or relax by receiving electrical impulses from the brain. They generally work in pairs; as one contracts, the other relaxes. The contracting muscle is the agonist and its partner the antagonist (or protagonist). The contraction/relaxation relationship between the two muscles is known as 'reciprocal inhibition'. The rate at which muscles change length is monitored by sensory spindles and sent to the brain. When the full length of the muscle is reached or a rapid stretch is sensed then the muscle will contract to protect itself. This is known as the 'Myotatic' or 'Stretch' reflex. It is therefore recommended that all stretching is done slowly to help inhibit the reflex action.

The *passive* range is the absolute range – that is, the muscle is stretched as far as it will go. External forces are normally needed to reach this position. This external force could be a teacher or coach, or possibly gravity. The *active* range is governed by internal forces, i.e. muscle contraction and extension. This range generally works against gravity.

Passive   Active   Passive   Active

There are many techniques now available to increase flexibility. It is important to recognise what you are trying to achieve. It is possible to decrease the resistances of the muscle, tendon, ligament and joint capsules, and also to increase the strength of the opposing muscle groups, which will therefore increase the gymnast's active range. Both are desirable; the latter is more easily achieved.

Ballistic stretching

This technique relies on a dynamic movement, e.g. bouncing in splits or leg swinging. When the muscle stretches to a certain point near to its limit, it activates the stretch reflex and the muscle automatically contracts. If the initial dynamic movement is strong enough this causes a powerful contraction which could damage the soft tissue. The Chinese have used rhythmic ballistic stretching for many years with great success. They stretch the muscle close to its maximum and then vibrate the muscle. The physiology behind this technique is not clear but it certainly has had great effect.

Static stretching

A simple example of static stretching would be for a gymnast to put a joint through its maximum range and then allow gravity or some other external force to exert a pressure on that joint. After a while the muscle spindle response gradually subsides, allowing the muscle to lengthen.

If a tendon, ligament or joint capsule is put under stress there is also an increase in the tension opposing the stretch. If the stress is kept on, then there is eventually an increase in the length of the muscle, tendon, ligament or joint capsule.

Proprioceptive Neuromuscular Facilitation (PNF) stretching

There are two techniques of PNF stretching that can be used: passive and active. The idea is to use the agonist and antagonist muscles against one another. When one muscle contracts, the opposing muscle has to relax, and vice-versa. This is known as Reciprocal Inhibition (RI).

Active PNF stretching

An example of the active technique would be as follows. A gymnast contracts the agonist muscles of her right leg to raise it; at the same time she has to relax the hamstrings (RI). A teacher or coach then exerts an external resistance by holding the heel of the raised leg. The gymnast can now make an isometric contraction of the antagonist muscles by pressing down on the coach's hand. A contraction of about 6 seconds is required.

| Lift | External resistance | Isometric contraction |

The gymnast then relaxes for a moment before she starts to lift the leg higher and repeat the whole procedure. The cycle of contraction, external resistance, isometric contraction should be repeated three times – this seems to be the optimal number for greatest effect. One advantage of this technique is that whilst one muscle group is being stretched another is being strengthened.

Passive PNF stretching

The gymnast's leg is raised passively to near its full range by the teacher or coach, and an external resistance is applied to the heel. This will allow isometric contraction of the antagonist muscle to take place for about 6 seconds. Then the gymnast relaxes the muscles so that there is a lull in the stretch reflex sensing devices before the coach moves the leg through its passive range. The cycle then continues twice more.

When a gymnast first starts to undertake a flexibility programme the safest form of stretching is gravity-assisted. The external forces are constant and the gymnast can gauge her own pain tolerance. She can be near her maximum stretch position, be aware of it and make minor movements towards it. It is important that good body alignment is kept throughout the movement.

It has been known for gymnasts to stretch each other, but this could cause problems. Gymnasts would need careful instruction on what they were trying to achieve. They would need to be very strong to hold the body in correct alignment whilst stretching their partner's muscles. At the maximum stretch position, great care has to be taken not to overstretch and cause injury. PNF stretching would need even longer instruction and care. It would be safer for only the teacher or coach, or an experienced adult, to assist with any stretching using external forces. The gymnast's own body weight under gravity should be quite sufficient for her needs.

4 Diet and nutrition

A gymnast's energy output can be compared to that of a car. Petrol must be put into a car before it can perform. If it has the wrong grade of petrol its performance will suffer. A gymnast has to be fed before she can perform. Incorrect feeding may effect both performance in the short term and health in the long term.

For the body to function normally it must take in various quantities of nutrients, i.e. carbohydrates, fat, protein, vitamins and minerals, plus fibre and water. All of these can be found in food. There is no one type of food that can cater for everything, hence the idea of a 'balanced diet', a mixture of foods containing a mixture of nutrients. Ideally the body should be in 'energy balance' too, so that food energy in = work energy out. This way weight will be neither gained nor lost.

Carbohydrates, especially complex or starchy carbohydrates, are a good source of energy. They can be found in rice, pasta, cereal, bread and vegetables. Starchy carbohydrates are often sources of other nutrients, too, especially B vitamins. In contrast, simple sugary carbohydrates such as those found in confectionery and sweetened drinks provide energy only; they rarely supply other nutrients.

Fat is a back-up source of energy for the body. It can be found in vegetable fats and oils, dairy foods including eggs, red meat, oily fish, confectionery and, of course, in foods cooked in or with any of these.

Protein is used in the growth and repair of the body and for most chemical reactions within the body. If more is eaten than is required for use in bodily tissues, it can also be converted into energy or stored as fat. Protein can be obtained from animal products (meat, fish, poultry, dairy foods) or certain vegetables such as peas, beans or nuts.

Vitamins regulate the vital body processes. There are two types, water-soluble (B and C) and fat-soluble (A, D, E and K). If you take in more water-soluble vitamins than you need they are simply excreted. Extra fat-soluble vitamins are deposited in the liver and may prove toxic. A 'balanced diet', including fresh fruit and vegetables daily, will provide the necessary balance, but if a gymnast is reducing energy intake then one multi-vitamin iron tablet per day is recommended.

Minerals are important in small amounts for the structure and function of the body. Calcium is needed to develop and maintain healthy bones. It can be found in milk and other dairy products. Potassium compounds

Svetlana Boginskaya, USSR

help to remove extra heat from an exercising muscle which may alleviate cramp. They can be found in fruits and vegetables. Magnesium compounds assist in carbohydrate breakdown to energy. They can be found in nuts, whole grain bread, bran cereals, and brown rice. Zinc compounds assist in muscle cell development. They can be found in whole grains, poultry, and red meat. Iron compounds are *very important*. They help carry oxygen to the body's cells. They can be found in liver, fish and meat, and in green vegetables. Shortage of iron due to menstrual losses may be a problem on an energy-restricted diet. Lethargy and lack of energy are the classic signs of anaemia or iron deficiency. Again, the multi-vitamin iron tablet mentioned earlier will help – but if any gymnast thinks she is anaemic, she should visit her GP.

Fibre is the indigestible part of the plant cell wall. It provides roughage which is needed to regulate the transit time of the faeces. It can be found in beans, bran, cereals, and whole grain products.

Water is a vital body constituent which is constantly being lost in both urine and perspiration. Dehydration can have a detrimental effect on performance, so it is essential to replace fluid in the body before you actually feel thirsty. Practice drinking little and often before and during training to ensure your fluid levels are topped up. Fluid intake regulates body temperature. Water and blood carry oxygen and nutrients to cells and transport waste products from the body.

Carbohydrates, fats and protein are the three nutrients which produce energy. When a body starts to exercise carbohydrates are called upon first, followed by the fats and then protein. There are complex biochemical reactions (Kreb's Cycle) which take these nutrients and convert them into a compound called adenosine triphosphate (ATP). This ATP breaks down to release energy.

Energy can be formed anaerobically (without oxygen) or aerobically (with oxygen), but only carbohydrates, in the form of glucose, can be converted into energy without oxygen. Since the competitive sport of women's gymnastics demands performances of only up to 90 seconds long, the major energy system used is anaerobic – and that means that a certain intake of carbohydrates is vital. It has been a fallacy for many years in gymnastics that food should be anything but potatoes, rice, bread, etc. In fact, these foods provide the right kind of fuel for the body to perform in this particular sport. In other sports, of course, there may well need to be a much more even balance between carbohydrates and fats, because the demands of the sport may well be aerobic, where the energy output is 300 times that of anaerobic exercise. As a rule of thumb, gymnasts should aim to be eating a ratio of 65% complex carbohydrates : 20% fats : 15% protein.

There are many reasons why female gymnasts should stay as light as possible for competition and only a *little heavier* for training. The extra weight of fat on the body can cause injury to the joints on take-off and landing from the apparatus. The more fat on the body, the less flexibility there is at a joint because of the layer of fat. Also, a lithe body is aesthetically more pleasing than one carrying fat. A light-framed person can handle more repetitions than a heavy-framed one, thus increasing the possibility of learning skills.

5 Mechanics

Many of those involved in teaching or coaching find the subject of mechanics confusing to the point where they switch off and coach from the heart. The terminology can be difficult, but the principles are not. Sound coaching can only be done with a sound knowledge of the principles of mechanics. This chapter explains the most important principles as straightforwardly as possible.

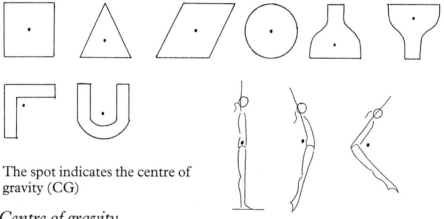

The spot indicates the centre of gravity (CG)

Centre of gravity

It is the gravitational pull of the earth that gives the gymnast's mass its weight. This external force is always present and acts towards the earth.

The centre of gravity (CG) is the point through which the weight of the body can be considered to act. This point can be inside the mass of the body or outside, depending on the shape the body is in at a particular moment.

Parabolic curve

A parabola is the name of the characteristic shape of the pathway that a gymnast's CG follows during flight. The exact shape of the parabola will be determined by the direction in which the gymnast's CG is travelling, and the velocity of the gymnast's CG before take-off.

Whilst in the air the gymnast can change her shape and therefore the distribution of the mass about the CG, but the flight path of the CG will be unaffected unless acted upon by some external force.

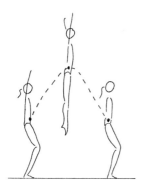 

Newton's First Law of Motion

'A body at rest will remain at rest, and a body in motion will remain in motion in a straight line and at a constant speed unless acted upon by an external force.'

In other words, a body will only accelerate if an unbalanced force is acting on it.

Force

Force is an influence which can cause a body to accelerate (gain velocity), decelerate (lose velocity) or change shape. Another definition would be: 'A force is that which alters or tends to alter a body's state of rest or of uniform motion in a straight line' (James G. Hay, *The Biomechanics of Sports Techniques,* 1985). For example, the force of a gymnast landing on the bed of a trampoline will cause the springs holding the bed to stretch (change shape). The built-in shape and the material of the springs will then cause the springs to contract (change shape), move the bed of the trampoline and throw the gymnast into the air. Because the springs are changing shape and creating forces, the gymnast decelerates as she hits the bed and accelerates as she leaves it.

Equal, balanced forces have no net effect on the body. For example, if one person pushes another in the chest whilst a second person pushes them in the back with the same force, there will be no movement. But if one pushes harder than the other, then there is acceleration in the direction of the stronger push.

Newton's Second Law of Motion

'When a force acts on a body, the body's centre of gravity (CG) will be accelerated in the direction of the force with an acceleration proportional to the magnitude of the force and inversely proportional to the mass of the body.'

This can be rewritten as Force = Mass × Acceleration. For instance, if two gymnasts jump into the air using the same force from the floor, but one is twice as heavy as the other, the heavier one will accelerate from the floor at half the rate of the lighter.

Force (100) = Mass (20) × Acceleration (5)
Force (100) = Mass (10) × Acceleration (10)

As far as gymnastics is concerned, this means that the greater the force and the lighter the body, the greater will be the increase in the body's motion. This is one good reason for conditioning the muscles to be stronger so as to create larger forces, and for the gymnast's weight to be kept in check.

Newton's Third Law of Motion

'For every action force there is a simultaneous reaction force, equal in magnitude but opposite in direction.'

If a gymnast were free in space, forces created by the body could only re-distribute the mass of the body about its centre of gravity; that is, only the shape could be changed. But if the gymnast is on the ground or on apparatus etc., and she exerts a force against the ground or apparatus, then the ground in turn exerts a reaction force of the same amount on the gymnast at the same time. Exerting a force on a fixed object results in movement away from it.

Vector diagrams

Forces can be represented by lines. The length of the line shows the magnitude of the force. The direction of the arrow indicates the direction of the force. The tail of the arrow is placed at the point of action of the force.
  If two forces are acting in the same direction on the same body they can be added together and represented by one line going in one direction. Conversely, if two forces are opposing one another they can be subtracted from each other and again can be represented by one line, as shown below.

Parallelogram of forces

In the sport of gymnastics, very few forces act just horizontally, so it is not always so easy to calculate the net effect of two forces. There is a method, however, that enables the net effect of two forces to be calculated regardless of the directions in which they act. The technique of calculation involves the use of parallelograms. In a parallelogram the opposite angles and sides have to be equal and the sides have to be parallel. The diagram below shows a parallelogram with two forces acting from corner A (lines A–B and A–D). The forces are acting in different directions, as the arrows show, and are of different magnitudes, as shown by the varying lengths of the lines. To work out the force that will result from these two forces and the direction in which it will be acting, the other two sides of the parallelogram have to be drawn. The resultant force will now be the diagonal of the parallelogram (line A–C) and this will also decide its direction.

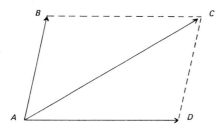

The representation of forces in diagrams

To keep models as simple as possible the forces are broken down into their vertical and horizontal components. In most models it is not the *forces* which are drawn on the diagram, but rather the opposite and equal *reaction forces*. The diagram on p. 36 shows the forces and reaction forces acting on a gymnast landing from a forward jump. The actual forces are F1 (the vertical component of the force), F2 (the horizontal component of the force) and Fr (the resultant or actual force). The unbroken lines show the forces that are acting upon the gymnast, i.e. the equal and opposite forces. F3 is the vertical component, F4 the horizontal component and Fr1 the resultant force.

The only other force acting on the body is that of gravity (Fg). This acts on the whole body, but for analysis purposes it is shown as acting through the centre of gravity of the body (CG).

On landing, the force Fr1 is acting behind the CG and not through it, and Fg is acting downwards. If the gymnast rebounds from the floor then her CG will be the point of rotation (forward). If the gymnast does not leave the floor then the feet will be the point of rotation and Fg will act outside the feet, causing forward rotation about the feet.

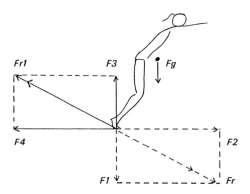

Linear and angular motion

Linear motion is motion in a straight line, and can occur in any direction. If a gymnast were free in space and a horizontal force were applied through the CG, the result would be a horizontal movement in the direction of the force and with no rotation.

If a force were to be applied at an angle of 45° through the point of the CG, the result would be a movement in the direction of the force, i.e. 45°.

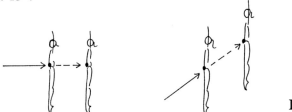

Linear motion

Angular motion occurs when a body moves in a circular pathway about a point or axis. The human body will always rotate about a line drawn through its CG. As we have just seen, if the force acts directly through the CG (concentric force) there is no rotation. However, when a force is applied to the body but does *not* act through the CG (eccentric force), then this creates rotation. The further the force is from the axis of rotation around the CG, the greater the angular motion around the axis of rotation.

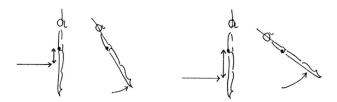

Angular motion

When analysing forces that relate to the gymnast in the air or at take-off, the CG of the body is the point of rotation. Whichever part of the body leaves the floor or apparatus last is where the forces should be directed. This tends to keep things simple. When the gymnast is circling a bar or has not left the ground (e.g. a handstand forward roll), then this contact point will be the axis of rotation.

Axes of rotation

There are three principal axes of rotation in airborne skills, which all act through the gymnast's CG. These are the lateral (transverse), anterior-posterior and longitudinal axes.

1. *Lateral (transverse) axis.* The backward and forward saltos work through this axis.
2. *Anterior-posterior axis.* Side saltos work through this axis.
3. *Longitudinal axis.* Twisting skills work through this axis.

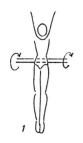 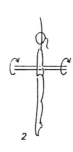  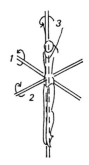

Twists

It is important to understand the principles of twisting, since they play a major part in the analysis of many elements. There are basically three types of twist. They have many names, the most popular being torque, cat and tilt twist.

Twist technique 1: torque twist

This technique uses a ground reaction force (or equipment reaction force), e.g. jump full twist.

The gymnast creates a force (F) in one direction (clockwise), a certain distance (d) from the point of rotation. The reaction force (F1) will create the twist in the opposite direction (anti-clockwise). Other than the anchor point, all other parts of the body turn in the direction of the intended twist. The greater 'd' becomes (within reason), the greater will be the force and therefore the twist.

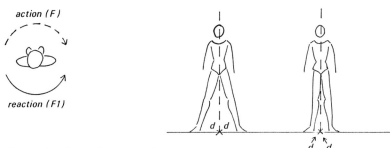

Twist technique 2: cat twist

Known also as zero-angular momentum twist, or body extension twist.

If a cat were dropped to the floor, back first, it would twist and land on its feet. There would be no ground reaction force or rotational force used to produce this twist. It happens by a complicated technique using Newton's Third Law of Motion (action-reaction). The cat moves one half of its body in one direction whilst the other half goes in the other direction. By varying the moments of inertia (the resistance of a body to changes in its motion), the cat will twist to land on its feet. It will first bring its upper body as close to the line of twist as possible, at the same time making its lower body spread out as far from the line of twist as possible. Because the upper body now has a smaller moment of inertia than the lower body it will rotate further, so that the upper body now faces the ground. If the whole situation is reversed, the lower body will rotate further than the upper body, with the result that the cat lands on its feet.

Another zero-angular momentum twist can be seen when a person rotates a hulahoop, or performs a seat drop swivel hips on the trampoline (seat drop extend, then half turn to seat drop). Rotation of the hips in one direction produces a rotation of the whole body in the opposite direction. This has to happen to maintain zero-angular momentum, as can be seen when the action is made whilst hanging from a rope suspended from the ceiling.

Twist technique 3: tilt twist

The third way of initiating twist is dependent upon rotation. If there is no rotation and a twist occurs, then this technique has not been used.

There used to be controversy over how twist occurs during rotation; was it by unequal radius initiation (e.g., lengthening one side of the body whilst shortening the other) or by tilting the body off its transverse axis and thereby creating twist? The latter finally won the day.

If a gymnast were performing a straight back salto with her arms above her head, and whilst in flight she lowered one arm to her side, there would be a redistribution of the body's mass about the CG. Newton's Third Law of Motion (action-reaction) applies, and the tilt occurs.

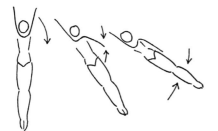 

Whilst the gymnast performs this move her body will be tilted; if she does not correct the tilt before she lands, then she will take a step or even fall sideways. It is important that when the twist is finished the arms should reverse their path back to the original position so that the tilt is corrected and the gymnast has centralised her CG ready for the landing.

6 Factors influencing learning

The sport of gymnastics is not only about the physical. There are many psychological factors which contribute to good performances in training and in competition. It is important for the teacher and coach to understand these factors. One of the most basic is the way in which gymnasts learn a skill. Learning can only be taking place if an improvement or change in performance is retained. A 'one-off' success does not necessarily mean that something has been learned.

Short and long loop feedback

For a gymnast to learn a skill, she must first understand what is being asked of her. This can be done by either a verbal or visual instruction. Once this information is in her memory it has to be sorted to determine what response is required. When this has been decided the brain sends commands via the central nervous system to the parts of the body necessary to achieve the required result. Even whilst this is happening, 'short' and 'long' loop feedback are occurring, up to the next and highest levels of command, to see if any minor corrections are needed through the movement.

If a gymnast took off for a somersault and her foot slipped, then the short loop feedback would take immediate action whilst the long loop feedback would eventually make the performer consciously aware that something had gone wrong and a correction had been made.

If a gymnast is taught to perform a skill with very little variation she will be able to reproduce the skill with high consistency, but only in a familiar context. If she were taught varied techniques, her general memory would allow her to perform moves in different environments. If a move is practised in different contexts the knowledge gained is relevant to other contexts, some of which may not even have happened yet.

There are some fundamental psychological skills which are very important to the learning process. They are goal-setting, concentration and attention control, self-regulation, imagery, verbalisation and the use of feedback. You must understand something of how they work and how to train your gymnasts in their use, in order to perfect the learning process.

Aurelia Dobre, Romania

Goal setting

It is important for the gymnast to have a clear understanding of what she is being asked to achieve. Equally the planned level of achievement must be realistic, attainable and controllable. Great skill is needed on your part to help gymnasts set goals which you both agree are attainable. If the gymnast doesn't believe that the goal can be attained, then it is pointless to continue the exercise. If you don't believe that the goal can be attained in the time available, then it is highly likely that the gymnast will get very anxious and frustrated as the deadline approaches, and again, she is unlikely to attain the goal. Both parties must agree to the goal.

The goal should also be controllable; that is, it should not rely on factors outside the gymnast's control. Setting a goal of 'winning the competition', for example, depends not only on the gymnast's own ability, but on that of the other performers and on the judges' decisions. A preferable goal would be 'performing four clean routines'. The only person who can affect this outcome is the gymnast, and if she achieved this goal then there would be every chance that she would win the competition as well.

Verbalisation

Verbal persuasion can be positive or negative. It has been overworked by some coaches, and instead of improving the gymnast's self-confidence and reducing her anxiety, it then becomes a harassment. When coaches shout at performers, things are generally going wrong. At this point, when the gymnast is already anxious and losing her self-confidence, shouting about mistakes or telling her to concentrate harder will only make things worse. Verbal persuasion should be about encouragement and directed towards helping the gymnast believe that she can achieve the goals set because they are realistic.

Feedback

Feedback for the performer can come in many forms. There is intrinsic feedback, which comes from the gymnast herself: she saw the end result and made mental corrections. It is possible to hear the a-bar twang or listen to the take-off for a move; as long as the gymnast knows what it is supposed to sound like, then corrections can be made. Again, it is possible to feel if something is going right. Was there enough pressure on the hands or should there have been more? If a gymnast knows that a somer-sault should land in a particular way or shape and she achieves this, then the knowledge gained from this result will help her achieve another move. There are two types of feedback here, knowledge of results and knowledge of performance.

There is also extrinsic feedback, from outside the gymnast. The coach can verbalise his or her knowledge of the perfected move in relation to the attempts of the gymnast. Some experimental data suggests that the more accurate the feedback, the quicker the progress that is made towards the ultimate goal; other such data suggests that the mental levels responsible for handling precise verbal instruction and those responsible for implementing it are too far apart to make this very effective. What is clear is the fact that verbal instruction will get the skill about right, and is therefore very valuable early on in learning a move and when things go badly wrong. Fine tuning, however, must be left to the individual gymnast. Suggestions can be made about where she might focus her attention, but asking gymnasts to make very small adjustments usually results in either no correction at all, or a very large and crude correction.

Too much feedback can have a negative effect. It is better to watch several attempts before offering advice. Taking one aspect of the performance and commenting on it, rather than commenting on every aspect, is likely to be much more beneficial.

The timing of feedback is also important. When the gymnast has just completed a move she will need time to analyse her own intrinsic information before she can accept verbal information from outside. A delay of about 10 seconds would be advantageous when giving feedback, unless you are simply going to shout 'good' or some other form of verbal praise. It takes great self-discipline to hold your comments for this length of time, especially if other coaches are around and offer unsolicited advice.

Personalities and emotions

Learning can, and will be, affected by how the teacher or coach sees him/herself and the performer and also by how the performer sees herself and you. It would be unrealistic to say that your role as teacher or coach is only to impart knowledge to the gymnast. You must be an instructor, motivator, disciplinarian, manager, administrator, publicity agent, social worker, friend, scientist and student, all in one. To be effective as an imparter of knowledge you must know yourself, your performer and your sport.

How well do you know yourself? You must have strengths and weaknesses; can you recognise them in yourself? All coaches and gymnasts are unique and should be treated as such. When you go into a gym your mood is very quickly picked up by the gymnasts and tends to be reflected in their work. When you go to a prestigious competition for the first time, how will you react? Will you be nervous, or too 'laid back'? Anxious and over-excited reactions will lead to mistakes, but attempts to appear calm and relaxed can be interpreted as lack of interest. It is always useful to talk to other teachers and coaches to see how they have handled such situations.

To be a good teacher or coach requires total commitment. It is your job to ensure that everything that needs to be done to bring about success is done. Much emotional and mental energy is required. Not only should you work your gymnast physically, but also mentally. She will need counselling and advising on the sport and on her life generally. An agreement will need to be made between you and the gymnast's family. If there is a great deal of pressure from her home, and a lack of support, this will affect the coach's moods in the gym, have an effect on the gymnast and result in poor learning experiences (to say nothing of what will happen to your own family unit). All these points are significant influences upon the creation of a learning situation which brings about success.

You need to know your performer, not only in the gym but out of it as well. All gymnasts are individuals. It is useful to assess their ability. If they are of a recreational standard it would be foolish to encourage them to set goals of World Championships level; be realistic and help them to set attainable goals. The gymnast will be happier, her parents will know where they stand and there will be no feelings of failure to make the grade, with tantrums in the gym, and so on. It is also important to know how each gymnast will react in certain circumstances. Will a new move excite her or make her anxious? Will competition make her nervous? What will relax her and enable her to perform better? Will it be mental rehearsal, or physical relaxation; can she mentally relax or should she just sit and talk about other things to take her mind off the task in front of her? It is important to know the performer and her likely reactions to different circumstances so that you can anticipate the situation and try to guide the gymnast through the experience with positive results.

It is also important to know your gymnasts as people. Do they have boyfriends, go to discos, like art or music? Do they have other talents that they wish to develop? What is their commitment level to the gym and other things in life? What are their eating habits? This has a direct effect on performance. Get to know their expectations of you and vice-versa.

It must be recognised that sometimes the personality of a teacher or coach and that of a gymnast are just not compatible. It is no one's fault, it is just a part of life. In this situation it is better for all concerned for someone else to coach the gymnast.

Motivation

There are basically two types of motivation, intrinsic and extrinsic, i.e. from within and from outside. When gymnasts first enter the gym, at some tender age, either someone else – probably their parents – has motivated them to go or they have themselves felt the wish to go. Normally, the coach is the great motivator in the gym. He/she encourages, chastises, puts situations together where the gymnast becomes inquisitive, and puts others together which intrigue and spur her on. There are times when gymnasts just enjoy the work, the group they are in and the pleasure they get from it. One of the most effective motivators is competition. Most gymnasts get very excited over the thought of little controlled competitions in the training gym; sometimes against themselves, sometimes against others and sometimes against the stop watch or tape measure.

Kudos is a great motivator. Gymnasts work very hard to get into a squad, whether it be club, county, regional or national. Once they are in one squad then the carrot is the next squad. When they have reached a squad, then representative honours can be a motivator. Squad companionships can be motivators. Not only do the gymnasts work hard and enjoy the work, but meeting fellow competitors from other clubs and training together, catching up on gossip, comparing notes, etc. are all part of the drive.

Generally, the teacher or coach is the main motivator until the age of puberty, when it becomes even more important for you to know your gymnasts inside and outside the gym so as to understand what makes them tick. Sometimes you will need to motivate the gymnast using things which are not directly associated with the gym, which makes the gymnast feel that you have bothered to go out of your way to find out something about them outside gymnastics. Respect in itself is a great motivator. As soon as the gymnast gets some success, whether it be learning a new move, achieving a performance goal, winning a medal, representative honours, pictures in newspapers, gymnast of the year or whatever, the external motivation from the coach diminishes a little and the intrinsic motivation of the individual takes over. Gymnasts seem to work longer, and when things are going wrong it can be the memory of that success that pulls them through the bad patch. Even conditioning almost becomes a pleasure, but even if it wasn't they would still do it.

With adolescence come the thoughts and attractions of boys. These are natural feelings and should not be discouraged. Used the right way they too can be a motivator. Boys in a gym training alongside girls can have a very positive effect if the situation is set up correctly. When the girls are having a bad session for one reason or another the boys can often get them out of the gloom and on the road again to positive gymnastics.

One of the greatest motivators for gymnasts, probably greater than competition and winning, is the announcement that they are going to learn a new move. Even in the competition season it is well worth while keeping a couple of new moves ticking over just for the motivation factor alone. On the other hand, ambitious, aggressive coaches or teachers, or those with huge egos which need to be satisfied at the expense of the gymnast, can have a very detrimental and de-motivating effect on the gymnast. Over-zealous parents who force their children to the gym for reasons of their own will also have a poor effect on the gymnast. A positive parent is one who stays at the gym long enough to show the gymnast that he/she is interested in the work the gymnast is doing, but who also has their own life to lead apart from that of their child. Many children resent the fact that their gymnastics is changing the normal running of their family life, and this can be a de-motivator.

As gymnasts get older and wiser, scores can become more important to them. As they go through the competition season they begin to formulate an average score for a certain performance, and an inaccurate score by the judges can sometimes distract them, even if the scores are too high! It is up to you to educate the gymnast about values. Correct scores are important, but the gymnast should be more concerned about satisfying herself and her coach, and achieving the goals set for that particular competition – attainable goals which are under her control. Scores are necessarily dependent upon the judges' subjective analysis of a performance. These scores may not necessarily reflect the true performance of the gymnast, and the gymnast may then become disheartened and lose the competition for reasons outside her control. It is much better for both gymnast and coach to be in control of their destiny, to choose and agree their own goals and play down the importance of scores as a means to an end. It may also be useful for you to give the gymnast your own idea of the score, which may alleviate some of her distress if the final score is very different from what was expected.

Many of the examples mentioned here can have a positive influence on the gymnast, but they can also quite easily have a negative one. It is very important that you get to know your gymnasts as quickly and as well as possible, so that the situations which present themselves can be directed towards the positive, thereby enhancing the gymnasts' motivation and the quality of their experience of gymnastics.

Mental rehearsal

In the club situation it is very difficult to get gymnasts to concentrate on that you have just said and to put it into practice at the next attempt. It is much easier for them to talk about last night's television or what is happening on another piece of apparatus, and so on. It can help to keep the gymnast's attention if you give the session more structure, and this also tends to achieve success more quickly. One way of doing it is to incorporate mental rehearsal. When the gymnast has completed her attempt at a certain move and has received the necessary feedback, ask her to mentally rehearse the correction, say ten times, before it is her turn again. This will give her something positive to concentrate on, increase the chances of success, help with the discipline of the session and allow less distraction by others. Mental rehearsal is a skill and needs to be taught like any other skill. Start with simple concepts which she can relate to and then go on to more difficult ones. For example, ask the gymnast to stand with her arms straight above her head. Get her to look at her arms to see that they are straight. Then ask her to imagine turning upside down and doing a handstand. Get her to check mentally that her arms are straight. Then ask her to attempt the handstand and make the physical feelings and mental pictures of the straight arms the same.

Too much emphasis is frequently placed on the physical abilities and not enough on the mental potential of the gymnast. Mental imagery is a powerful tool if used correctly. Once this technique has been harnessed in training, it can be taken to the competition arena and used with great effect. Many good gymnasts have lost competitions because they have not developed their mental skills to help deal with a very pressurised environment.

7 The prudent coach: legal considerations*

Hazel Wearmouth

You will be familiar with the constitution, rules and regulations, codes of practice and procedures of the BAGA, which were established partly to reflect, reinforce and formalise those things about gymnastics which you value and wish to perpetuate and protect. Formal rules imply equality of opportunity, justice and fairness, and remind participants of their obligations as human beings to respect and protect each other. If this does not appear always to work in practice, then perhaps we should rigorously appraise both the rules themselves and the ethos and values which surround them.

The laws of the land, like the rules of your sport, are intended to regulate the conduct of both teachers and pupils, and you should examine your practices in the light of both the spirit and the letter of the law.

The ways in which the law affects gymnastics are numerous, and include the following:

- Civil law (e.g. negligence)
- The Health and Safety at Work Act (1974)
- Employment law
- Disciplinary procedures, codes of conduct
- Equal opportunities, including sex discrimination[1]
- Fire regulations
- Music copyright

However, in the context of this chapter, it will be sensible to concentrate on outlining the civil law tort of negligence because of its central role for *the prudent coach*, as covered in Class 4 of the BAGA Common Core Syllabus.

* I should like to thank Colin Still for the opportunity to make a small contribution to this volume. In writing this chapter I have responded to a brief to provide material on the general theme of *The prudent coach* in gymnastics, providing a basic framework which could act as a 'springboard' (well supported by references) for further study and development. I hope this will help teachers and coaches who face greater responsibilities and potential dilemmas as they develop and progress.

I should also like to thank Professor Margaret Talbot, Valerie Collins and Leslie Pike for their invaluable support in reading and commenting on various drafts of this chapter.

Full twisting Yurchenko vault: Olga Strajeva, USSR

Physical educators (and coaches) must understand the legal framework within which they plan and conduct their programmes. An informed employee (or coach) is one who understands legal liability, particularly negligence; the standard applied by the courts; the manner in which the court reaches its decisions in such cases; and the defences available to the defendant (employee/employers) in a negligence case.[2]

A person who has been injured whilst taking part in gymnastics may seek financial compensation if he or she can show that the injury was a result of somebody being negligent. However, teachers and coaches often worry unduly since they assume, first, that *any* injury in the gym will almost certainly lead to a civil suit against them; and second, that the law has expectations of them which are totally incongruent with standard and approved practices in gymnastics. The first thing to point out, therefore, is that the law expects not that you should be a *perfect* teacher or coach, but that you should be a *reasonable* (prudent) one. A claim for negligence will be successful *only* if the following conditions are met:

1. A *duty of care* must be owed by the defendant to the plaintiff (i.e., the gymnast).
2. There must be a breach of that duty of care,
3. *Thereby* causing actual damage to the plaintiff.

Although we shall look at the first and third conditions, the main focus of this chapter will be an examination of what constitutes 'duty of care' in terms of 'standard of care' (condition 2) in the context of gymnastics.

1 What is a duty of care?

The key to understanding the duty of care is the 'neighbour principle', established in *Donoghue* v. *Stevenson* (1932).

> You must take reasonable care to avoid acts and omissions which you can reasonably foresee would be likely to injure your neighbour where 'neighbour' seems to be 'persons who are so closely and directly affected by my act that I ought reasonably to have them in contemplation as being so affected when I am directing my mind to the acts or omissions which are called into question'.[3]

It is normally assumed that anyone teaching or coaching an activity owes a duty of care to the participants. BAALPE (1985) advises that 'The duty of care relationship exists whenever children are in pursuit of school-sponsored activity with teachers (coaches) present, even in a voluntary capacity.'[4]

2   There must be a breach of that duty of care

Difficulties can arise in trying to establish the standard of care expected of a gymnastics teacher or coach and in assessing each case for any breach of that duty. 'Negligence is a conduct which fails to conform to a standard required by law for safeguarding others or oneself against reasonable risk of injury.'[5] The law cannot and will not be specific regarding this standard. However, there are general principles which are applied to each specific case, and several levels of expectation operate.

1.   Any teacher owes the charges in his or her care (if children) a duty to take the care one would expect of reasonably prudent parents.[6]
2.   The standard of care expected increases in the case of a qualified/ professional person (a gymnastics coach or teacher): you are expected, as a result of your training and experience, to visualise the results of your acts in a particular sphere (gymnastics) and to be prepared for and guard against the likelihood of children unknowingly creating potentially dangerous situations. Collins advised teachers to consider the following factors:

- The age of the person (higher standard of care necessary with children)
- The expertise and experience of the participants (less experienced gymnasts require more care)
- The more dangerous the activity, the greater the care you are expected to exercise
- The likelihood of an injury occurring
- The suitability of the particular premises/equipment for the activity concerned.[7]

The 'reasonable standard of care' expected of you as a gymnastics coach or teacher can be partly represented by 'standard and approved practice'. Standard or *common* practice is not enough; it must be *approved* by official sources. BAALPE (1985) described it in this way: ' ... where a practice has been commonly adopted by teachers (coaches) throughout the country and has proved by time and experience to be safe and efficient'.[8] Sources of standard and approved practice in gymnastics are normally associated with, but not restricted to, BAGA approved coaching courses. When evaluating the conduct of a gymnastics teacher or coach involved in a negligence claim, the courts might refer to textbooks, manuals, videos and expert witnesses representing 'the official line'. 'Standard and approved practice' covers all aspects of your work with gymnasts.

'Standard and approved practice' is not written in tablets of stone, and the official view of what is safe practice may change; it is important that you keep up-to-date with current thinking, discussing and sharing your views with others in the profession, avoiding isolation. Professor R. W. Rideout advises: 'The more safety practices that get about, the less risk is inherent in the sport and so, in a sense, you are constantly upgrading the standard that is being applied to you.'[9] In the case of *Conrad* v. *ILEA*,[10] a participant was injured whilst being thrown by a partner in his very first judo class, and the defendants were found to be negligent. They appealed, on the grounds that, according to expert witnesses, at the time of the injury, standard and approved practice in judo coaching was in fact changing to incorporate the increasingly accepted earlier introduction of throwing techniques. The court of appeal found for the defendants, and the decision was reversed.

Reference to good practice in gymnastics may be augmented by Health and Safety codes of practice produced and implemented by employers and employees in a particular working context, e.g. local education authorities, leisure services, private sport/health facilities and institutional codes of practice, trade union Health and Safety policies, and those of the Department of Education and Science. You are advised to check the Health and Safety policy of your employer (it is your duty to know it and co-operate in its implementation). Some differences may exist between the different agencies employing gymnastics teachers and coaches as regards the procedures governing the use of particular rebound apparatus, supporting pupils, insurance cover, systems for reporting hazards, etc.

The reasonable standard of care partly reflected in following standard and approved practice is approached and packaged in many different ways by coach and teacher educators. It is not appropriate, or even advisable, to translate this generalised standard into a specific exhaustive list. However, Nygaard and Boone[11] have suggested a very general checklist of coach 'duties' which may help you to evaluate your conduct.

- Supervision
- Sound planning
- Warning of inherent risks of the activity
- Provision of a safe (and appropriate) environment
- Evaluation of gymnasts' capacity/incapacity to participate
- Fairly matching or equating participants (for training or competition)
- Provision of proper first aid and establishment of emergency medical procedures that can be immediately put into action

Let us now go on to examine these duties with some reference to English case law where relevant.[12] These guidelines are not exhaustive, and should be applied to each individual situation, using your own judgement.*

1   Supervision

Supervision must be adequate in a general and specific sense. *General supervision* involves the monitoring of the whole group, including assistants, parents, etc., in all gymnastic contexts, e.g. gymnasia, changing rooms,

*I am indebted to the work of Geoffrey Dunn on the development of Nygaard and Boone's framework.

travelling to and from venues, etc. *Specific supervision* involves a closer level of observation and control, e.g. supporting a gymnast through a skill. There are no set ratios for general supervision. However, obvious common-sense factors should be considered:

- Position yourself to observe all participants and respond promptly to hazards.
- The more dangerous the activity, the closer should be your supervision.
- Do not leave the group unattended or unobserved.
- *Only* use children for supporting if they have the knowledge and training to assist in that particular situation.[13]
- Follow agreed codes of practice for supervision, formal and casual use of facilities.
- Make sure all helpers are clearly briefed and all participants understand a clear STOP sign.

In *Wright* v. *Cheshire C.C.*,[14] an injury in vaulting had resulted from a pupil (who should have been supporting the next vaulter) running out of the gym at the sound of the school bell, and the teacher was found to have been negligent in allowing pupils to support each other. However, when the case reached the court of appeal the decision went in favour of the defendants on the grounds that (a) it was unforeseeable that the pupil would do this (it had never happened before), and (b) it was standard and approved practice for boys of this age and experience to support each other as long as they were prepared properly to cope with the responsibilities it involved.

Deviations from the planned activity due to changes in circumstances can often lead to a breakdown in the standard of supervision. Imagine this scenario ... A coach is absent (ill), so three groups are joined together in the gym. Two coaches supervise a conditioning circuit which involves a competition situation. There are six 'stations' or tasks, five of which are not made more dangerous by fatigue or the competitive atmosphere; the exception is a vault skill without specific support provided, where it is known that most of the group cannot complete the vault unsupported. One coach leaves the gym to attend to a discipline problem outside, and a participant (on the fourth circuit and tiring) falls from the vault and breaks an arm ...[15]

Supervision does not only involve monitoring hazards to gymnasts taking part in a session. Gymnastic equipment is hazardous but very attractive to children, visitors, trespassers, etc., and good security and adequate supervision should extend beyond the gymnastic session. For example, in *Beaumont* v *Surrey C.C.*, thick elastic removed from a trampette was discarded in a waste paper basket outside the gym. At breaktime, supervision from staff and prefects failed to materialise for ten minutes, by which time some eleven-year-old boys had removed the elastic from the bin and used it to project each other in a game which resulted in a boy losing the sight of one eye. The presence of this thick elastic in the open bin, together with a failure to provide adequate supervision, amounted to a failure to reach the expected reasonable standard of care.[16]

2   Sound planning

Sound planning can help you to reduce the number of risky situations. Well-thought-out lesson plans can help you to identify and reduce reasonably foreseeable harm that might arise out of incorrect use of space or equipment, inappropriate tasks or progressions, insufficient time allocated to skill learning and repetition. 'Poor planning increases the likelihood of poor execution. But even perfectly designed plans are of no value unless you carry them out in a reasonable and prudent fashion.'[17] It is worth paying particular attention to the following points:

- Prepare your plans according to standard and approved practice.
- Brief all assistants carefully, and avoid sudden deviations from such instructions.
- When planning, allow time for explanations, demonstrations, warnings, repetitions, orientation, etc.
- Work towards appropriate aims and objectives, including evaluation of plans.
- Be aware of the difference between a diagram and the apparatus actually laid out in the gym.

3   Warning of inherent risk

'Warning of risk' is not a well-developed practice in teaching and coaching in the United Kingdom. It is common practice, and a very formalised process, in the United States. Nygaard and Boone advise coaches to: 'Warn players of the inherent risks in the sport and of the dangers of using questionable techniques. Repeat these warnings regularly so that your players know, understand and appreciate the risks which they may encounter.'[18] The intention is to make the gymnasts understand, through these repeated warnings, their own responsibility to each other and to the coach to co-operate in confining the risks of gymnastics to inherent risks – that is, those irreducible risks that remain when all reasonable precautions have been taken.

   The warnings you give to your gymnasts should be written, clear, and comprehensive. Remember that the younger the child, the more care you will have to take to make sure the warnings are understood and remembered. If they are too young to appreciate or understand them, double check the normal procedure of informing parents of these risks.

4　Provision of a safe (and appropriate) environment

This is a *very* important duty, and one that links all the others. It relates to equipment and people as well as buildings and space.

Case histories cited by BAALPE (1985) identify common defects which could constitute a failure to reach a reasonable standard of care:

- Wet, slippery, cracked, dirty floors
- Unstable equipment
- Inappropriate footwear, stockinged feet, jewellery
- Holes on box tops
- Damaged or protruding electrical fittings
- Poorly arranged, worn or frayed mats
- Insufficient heating and poor lighting
- Cramped spaces or obstructed runways
- Cracked or broken windows

Bearing the above list in mind, critically examine your facility and equipment for potential and actual hazards. Adhere to obvious common-sense procedures, including the following:[19]

1. Gymnastics apparatus should conform to the British Standards Institute Standard and be inspected and repaired on a regular basis by a company which specialises in this work. Equipment should be inspected formally in this way every twelve months, but you should monitor it constantly yourself as it is used. 'Insecure or broken apparatus should not be used until the necessary repair work has been carried out. Such apparatus should be removed from the working area and clearly marked.'

2. Make sure equipment is used for the purpose for which it was designed (and in its original form). Any adaptations to equipment should be carefully checked by appropriate technical experts. The technical unit of the Sports Council keeps a record of such adaptations and is advised by the technical department of the BAGA.

3. Apparatus should always be checked before use, even if it was erected by someone else (e.g. sports centre staff).

4. Rules for the layout and use of equipment should be clear; assistants and gymnasts should be trained in the appropriate methods and be made aware of the dangers of incorrect use.

5. Runways should be unobstructed; floors should be non-slip and clean.

6. In multi-use facilities, e.g. games/gymnastics, gymnastics apparatus such as trampolines should be stored safely and locked away, not, for example, left around the edge of a basketball court.[20]

7. Access to potentially hazardous and tempting equipment and facilities should be prohibited when supervision is not available.

Apart from fire doors, all the doors to a facility should be kept locked when it is not in use.

8. Precautions against fire should be taken, in line with the appropriate regulations, and evacuation procedures should be regularly drilled. Fire extinguishers, hoses, etc., should be regularly checked.

9. Foam-based facilities should be evaluated in relation to the Home Office-issued Fire Services circulars no 1/1988 (FSC1/88) and SCFM87.[21]

10. Foam pits should be regularly checked for water seepage, vermin and dangerous objects; foam should be 'fluffed up' when it gets compressed, and the sides and edges of the pit should be well padded with a material specifically designed for that purpose and in a colour which will stand out from the floor and pit.

11. Gymnasts should be correctly dressed, e.g. non-slip shoes, no baggy tee-shirts, no jewellery, no chewing gum, and no clothing which would interfere with your ability to support.

You and your employer share the responsibility for seeing that these procedures are followed, and you should use the agreed 'system' in the written Health and Safety policy for reporting on and eliminating hazards.

5 Evaluation of gymnasts' capacity/incapacity to participate

Another area identified by Nygaard and Boone is the need to screen and monitor all gymnasts to establish if there are any reasons why participation would be inadvisable. You should:

• Screen all participants new to the group and record any medical problems, including any medication; you must be aware of any drugs they may be taking. Unsuitable candidates should be advised not to participate at all.

• Adhere to clear criteria and procedures for fitness testing, as to whether or not a gymnast should compete for example, in co-operation with the appropriate personnel, as laid down in BAGA policy or international federation rules where relevant.

• Take care during rehabilitation after injury to resist any pressure (including from the gymnast herself) to return to full participation too soon.

• Take account of physical, mental and emotional factors when assessing a gymnast's suitability for participation.

In 1981 a pupil with a known congenital hip defect injured her ankle whilst attempting a handstand during a gymnastics lesson.[22] The child's mother had informed the school of this defect and had made it quite clear that the girl should not participate in PE lessons, and this was noted in the school records. However, the girl was so keen to take part that she told the PE teacher that she could do so soon and turned up in her kit for the gymnastics lesson. She persuaded the teacher to let her take part, and suffered the injury. The school had an adequate system for recording such matters, but it was overridden in this case. Two points noted by Barrell and Partington about this case are that:

- If a parent has put some proper restriction on a child's activities, this restriction must be respected until the parent lifts it.
- If a child with a known or suspected disability is taking part in an unaccustomed activity, more rigorous supervision is required.[23]

6   Fairly matching or equating participants (for training or competition)

You must be absolutely sure that your gymnasts are not put at a serious disadvantage or placed in a situation where foreseeable harm might occur by poor matching of, for example, weight, height, skill, experience, maturity, age, mental state or (in mixed warm-ups) sex. (The main application of this guideline is obviously contact sports, but it might have implications for gymnastics as well.)

In 1984 a PE teacher playing rugby with fifteen-year-old boys momentarily forgot that they were smaller and weaker than himself, and he caused a serious spinal injury to one of his pupils when he tackled him. The courts found that the teacher was negligent. Whether or not this would necessarily have implications for other sports is not clear.[24] However, it does make it advisable for you to scrutinise such gymnastics practices as:

- Coach/leader participation in warm-up
- Partner matching in warm-up, conditioning games and skill practices
- Joining together individuals/groups of different ages and sexes for any part of the gymnastics programme

7   Provision of proper first aid and establishment of emergency medical procedures

You are not required to have the training or diagnostic ability of a doctor or paramedic, but you must have basic first aid skills and an organised system for obtaining skilled medical help if necessary[25] in all gymnastics contexts (training, competitions, displays, courses, travelling). Negligence *may* arise from (a) doing nothing; (b) doing the wrong thing; or (c) selecting the right course of action but performing it incorrectly. You are advised:

1.   To stay within your area of competence (i.e. basic first aid) and to stick to essentials, viz.:

- Stop class, assess situation.
- Take action to maintain life, protect from further harm and reassure the patient.
- Obtain skilled medical help if necessary and follow up (inform parents, inform supervisor, fill in accident forms, etc.).

2. To have available on the premises a named competent person and an adequate first aid kit. Check the kit regularly and replace missing or damaged items.[26]
3. Not to try to remove the injured gymnast from the area, especially if a head, neck or back injury is suspected; prevent any movement and get expert help.
4. To have an established plan for emergencies, including briefing of gymnasts, assistants and administrative staff.
5. To record all accidents in accordance with the Health and Safety policy. If classified as a dangerous occurrence, follow RIDDOR regulations.[27]

This list of seven areas structuring 'a reasonable standard of care' is not exhaustive, but together with reference to standard and approved practice it may provide a framework within which you can evaluate your own standards of care.

Defences against negligence

The defences against negligence may be summarised as follows:

1. The injury was a *genuine accident*. It was *unforeseeable* and could therefore not reasonably have been avoided.
2. No *duty of care* was owed by the defendant to the plaintiff (the injured gymnast).
3. '*Volenti non fit injuria*'. The gymnast voluntarily consented to the known risk of harm and cannot therefore claim compensation if that harm materialises. Three conditions must be present for this particular defence to apply, namely that the gymnast's consent was

   - Voluntary
   - Informed
   - Related to the inherent risk of the activity only [28]

4. *Contributory negligence.* Although contributory negligence is not strictly speaking a defence, damages awarded to an injured gymnast may be reduced if it can be shown that she was negligent and that this negligence contributed to the injuries suffered. (Cases outside sport where this defence has been successful include failure to wear car seat belts or crash helmets on motorbikes.) Difficulties arise in the case of younger children contributing to their own injury.[29]
5. One of the strongest defences against negligence is that *standard and approved practice was followed*.

6.   The conduct of the defendant (teacher/coach/employer) was not the *proximate cause of the injury,* i.e. the act/omission of another agent intervened and broke the chain of causation linking the injury of the gymnast with the action of the coach. Incorrect medical treatment at the hospital aggravating the injury would be an example of an intervention; a congenital disorder unknown to the coach causing the injury is another.

If all this sounds terribly familiar and in line with what you have been practising for years, it reinforces the point that the law does not expect perfection: it expects reasonableness, and what the law decides is reasonable depends heavily upon the body of 'standard and approved practice' built up over the years within the sport. It is not the avoidance of litigation which motivates you as a gymnastics coach to take reasonable care of your gymnasts – it is your genuine concern to protect participants from reasonably foreseeable harm, and this is exactly what the law expects and wishes to encourage.

If you wish to further your understanding of law and sport. I strongly recommend consulting V. Collins' *Recreation and the Law* [30] and E. Grayson's *Sport and the Law* [31] as well as the references listed below. In addition, at the time of writing the National Coaching Foundation consortium is preparing the Diploma in Professional Studies (Sports Coaching) for validation. It is planned to include work on the legal and ethical environments in which coaches and performers work.

References

1.   Talbot, M., 'The Sex Discrimination Act: Implications for the delivery of physical education, recreation and sport', in *Legal Liability and Physical Education* conference proceedings, Carnegie Department, Leeds Polytechnic, 2 November 1988.
2.   Arnold, D.E. (1985), 'Legal considerations in teaching physical education', in *Physical Education: Teacher Education. Guidelines for Sport Pedagogy,* ed. Lynn Venedien and J. E. Nixon, p. 46.
3.   *Donoghue* v. *Stevenson* (1932), C. A. 562 H. L., p. 580.
4.   British Association of Advisers and Lecturers in Physical Education (BAALPE), (November 1985), *Safe Practice in Physical Education,* p. 20 (being rewritten at present).
5.   Fleming, J. (1985), *An Introduction to the Law of Torts,* 2nd edn (Clarendon Law Series), p. 22.
6.   The doctrine of the careful parent, established by *Williams* v. *Eady* (1893), T.L.R. 637.
7.   Collins, V. (1988), 'Negligence and physical education', in *Legal Liability and Physical Education* conference proceedings, Carnegie Department, Leeds Polytechnic, 2 November 1988, pp. 3 – 4.
8.   BAALPE, *Safe Practice in Physical Education* (Chester, 1985), p. 26.
9.   Rideout, R.W., 'Codes of Practice: the Law, Health and Safety at Work', in *Safety in Sport: a cause for concern,* a seminar report (Association of

Polytechnic Physical Education Lecturers – APPEL), London, April 1987.

10. *Conrad* v. *ILEA* (1967). *The Times Law Report,* 29 November 1967, in Barrell, G.R. (1970), *Legal Cases for Teachers* (London, Methuen), pp. 276 – 95 (P.E.).

11. Nygaard, G. and Boone, T.H. *Coaches' Guide to Sport Law,* a publication for the American Effectiveness Programme, Level 2 Sport Science Curriculum (Champaign, Illinois, Human Kinetics Publishers Inc.), pp. 6 – 7.

12. NB Only 30% of cases are reported in the Law Journals. These are usually those cases which are of particular interest as a legal issue/principle and have reached the Court of Appeal. Only a small percentage of these cases will be sport-related. (Also, many claims are settled out of court.)

13. BAALPE, *Safe Practice in Physical Education,* p. 24.

14. *Wright* v. *Cheshire County Council,* (1952) 2. *ALL.E.R.* 789. For Court of Appeal, see Barrell, *Legal Cases for Teachers,* pp. 284 – 90.

15. An actual incident — case not settled yet.

16. *Beaumont* v. *Surrey* (1968), 66 *L.G.R.* 580; *LCT* 246. See Barrell, G.R. and Partington, J., *Teachers and the Law,* 6th edn (London, Methuen), pp. 376, 377.

17. Nygaard and Boone, *Coaches' Guide to Sport Law,* p. 19.

18. Nygaard and Boone, *Coaches' Guide to Sport Law,* p. 6.

19. For a comprehensive and thorough set of guidelines, see BAALPE, *Safe Practice in Physical Education,* pp. 37 – 42.

20. In 1980, a trampoline left out unattended in an unlocked sports hall resulted in the paralysis of a seventeen-year-old boy (a trespasser). The matter was settled out of court, awarding £40,000 to the boy (see Collins, 'Negligence and physical education').

21. Also see (1) foam-based sports recreation and play equipment factsheet; (2) 'Getting the Feel for Foam', 14-minute VHS video (Sports Council, 16 Upper Woburn Place, London WC1H 0QP).

22. *Moore* v. *Hampshire C.C.* (1982) 86. *L.G.R.* 481.

23. See Barrell and Partington, *Teachers and the Law,* on the above case (22).

24. See discussion of this case, *Affutu-Nartey* v. *Clarke and Anor,* before Mr Justice Hodgson: Q.B. Division 8.2. 1984, *The Times Law Report,* 9 February 1984, by E. Grayson, and *Safety First for Coaches* (1986), National Coaching Foundation, pp. 65 – 6.

25. Nygaard and Boone, *Coaches' Guide to Sport Law,* p. 69.

26. See (1) Health and Safety Executive, *First Aid at Work Regulations* (1981) (currently under review); (2) *Emergency Aid in the Workplace for Appointed Persons* ed. Bernard Lucas (for St John Ambulance Association and Brigade).

27. *A Guide to the Reporting of Injuries, Diseases and Dangerous Occurrences: Regulations* (1985), H.S.(R) 23, HMSO/RIDDOR, see section 3(i), p. 3, on people who are not themselves at work, the pupils/students, the public. Employers/institutions will have their own internal system of accident reporting, which at some level will involve evaluating the necessity to report the accident to the Health and Safety Executive.

28. For a critical analysis of 'volenti' in sport and physical education, see Wearmouth, H.J., *'Volenti non fit injuria' in sport and physical education,* in *Legal Liability in Physical Education* conference proceedings, Carnegie Department, Leeds Polytechnic, 2 November 1988.

29. Collins, V. 'Negligence and physical education'.
30. Collins, V. (1988), *Recreation and the Law* (London/New York, E. and F.N. Spon); Grayson, E., *Sport and the Law* (1988), London, Butterworth.
31. National Coaching Foundation, 1–3 College Close, Beckett Park, Leeds Polytechnic, Leeds LS6 3QS, Yorkshire.

8 Safety and responsibility

Maintenance of facilities

When a gymnast goes into a training facility she expects it to be totally safe and ready for use. For this to be so, the teacher or coach and the maintenance staff must make regular checks to minimise any risk to the gymnast. The factors to be considered which could cause harm to an individual are the building, the apparatus, other equipment, the teacher or coach and the gymnasts.

The building

Many clubs use buildings which were not purpose-built for gymnastics. A totally open space for the equipment would minimise accidents, since the variables are four walls and a ceiling. The construction of some gymnasia involves the use of supporting posts or pillars from the floor to the ceiling and protrusions from the wall. If this is the case then they should be padded, so as to give the gymnast some protection if she should make contact with them. The gym should also use colour to make objects stand out from their surroundings.

Some gymnasia have girders to support the roof. If so, then the positioning of the apparatus could become critical. Any trampoline, trampette, vault or set of bars would need to be positioned very carefully.

Many injuries are caused by low temperatures in the gym. A gymnast must be able to stand around in just a leotard for many hours without feeling cold, which causes a reduction to the blood circulation to the muscles. Temperatures of 19–21°C would not be unreasonable.

Lighting – or the lack of it – can also be the cause of some injuries. A well-lit diffused type of lighting is the most acceptable. Gymnasts may well mis-judge distances in low light and make incorrect adjustments when trying to see the springboard, horse, bar or beam.

Many gyms are now fitted with sunken pits, but they too can have their problems. Gymnasts take off from the edge of the pit or from a piece of apparatus over the pit. Either way, there is a risk of them hitting the side of the pit. This should therefore be covered with a material specifically designed for the purpose, and again colour should be used to ensure that it stands out from the foam and the floor.

Park Ji Sook, Korea

The foam in a pit is surrounded by air pockets and acts as a decelerator for the gymnast as she makes contact with it. The foam can get compressed after a while so that the gymnast decelerates too quickly, possibly causing injury. It is essential that the pit is frequently 'fluffed up' to keep the air in it. Periodically the pit itself must be checked to see if any water is getting in from outside, especially if it was dug beneath the water table line. If the foam gets waterlogged the water takes up air space and the gymnast decelerates too quickly, which may cause injury. Foam that looks dry on top may be full of water underneath. It has been known for a pit in this state to attract vermin and with it disease.

There are many types of foam. Some are now fire-rated on a scale from 1–5. It is recommended that level 5 foam, which resists ignition the longest, is used. If gymnasts inhale fumes from burning foam they could be breathing cyanide gas. It is essential that there are sufficient fire exits in the building.

The equipment

The siting of equipment is crucial. The dismount from any apparatus must be sufficient to ensure that the gymnast cannot hit the wall or any object that happens to be prominent.

Dependent on the usage of the equipment each year, periodical checks need to be made. Much of the equipment is made of nuts, bolts, screws, springs etc., which work themselves loose. Most of the equipment can be adjusted for different heights, and this is done in most training sessions, so each piece of kit should be inspected to make sure it is safe before any gymnast goes on to it.

Different types of matting are made for different jobs. Some decelerate the gymnast faster than others for specific reasons and are positioned in specific places. It is common for gymnasts to move mats around without realising their specific qualities and the reason they were placed in a certain position – a good reason for inspection.

Matting must be regularly checked for signs of deterioration. For example, safety landing modules tend to 'bottom out' very quickly with constant use. Gymnasts often believe that these mats will protect them under all circumstances, but this is not the case. Matting which is permanently left down will last much longer than that put away after each training session. The frequency of the checks must reflect this.

The teacher or coach

The sport of gymnastics demands a great deal of contact between the teacher or coach and the performer. It is essential that you wear correct attire so as to minimise the risk of injury both to the performer and to yourself. A pair of sandal-type shoes does not encourage speed or surefootedness, and might lead to an injury. A gymnastic slipper or training shoe is much more suitable. You should be aware of the material of the clothing which you and the performer are wearing. If both are wearing a synthetic material, the friction between them is greatly diminished. One day both coach and gymnast may be wearing cotton or woollen garments and there is no problem with supporting, and the next they could be wearing nylon garments and the gymnast would feel like a 'slippery bar of soap'.

Any kind of jewellery should be carefully scrutinised. Protruding rings, long necklaces, buckles, long earrings, watches and spectacles are all potential dangers, to both gymnast and coach.

Current fashions allow both men and women to have long or short hair. If a teacher or coach has long hair he or she must retain it in such a way that it does not get tangled up with the gymnast whilst she is being supported for a move. It is also dangerous for the coach's hair to impair his or her vision when about to support a gymnast.

Coaches and performers come in all shapes and sizes and it would be irresponsible for a small coach to try and support a large gymnast for particular moves. Some coaches are very experienced and highly co-ordinated, but even they would be foolish to try and support some gymnasts who are large and moving at great speed, because this produces a huge force which is not easily contained.

The gymnast

It is your responsibility to ensure that the gymnast is not wearing anything which may harm her during the training session.

When a gymnast is training on a trampoline or mini-tramp, she should wear something to cover her bare feet. The webbing of the bed which she is bouncing on could otherwise be dangerous, since a toe can be trapped between the webbing and seriously injure the gymnast.

On asymmetric bars the gymnast's hands create friction and heat whilst going around the bar. It is possible to buy bar grips to help alleviate much of the problem. Hand injuries may occur if they are not worn. It has to be said that injuries may arise even if they are worn, but at least there is some protection. Baggy tee-shirts are a great favourite with gymnasts for training in, but they also create problems. It is very difficult to see the form of the gymnast through the baggy tee-shirt, and therefore difficult to hand-spot her, let alone analyse her work. A more important consideration is that you may become ensnared in the billows of the garment whilst supporting, with disastrous results.

Jewellery should not be worn by the gymnast, especially if training into pits. When a gymnast lands in a pit any jewellery she is wearing tends to get snagged on the foam and be pulled or even ripped off. Not only is it difficult to find the lost items, but if not found they linger in the pit as a potential danger for the next gymnast.

Gymnasts with long hair have no option but to tie it back in such a way that they can see at all times and it cannot get caught up on the apparatus or on a coach providing support.

For gymnasts to train as safely as possible there must be a great deal of co-operation between them and the coach. If the planning of the building, the positioning of the kit, its maintenance and the people's clothing are all of the highest standard, then the risk of injury is much diminished.

9 Finance and management

This chapter is principally intended for club coaches, but some of the areas covered may, it is hoped, prove of interest to teachers too.

The club coach must work to a code of ethics, which will affect his or her decision-making when dealing with the club, the gymnasts and their parents, and society in general. Many situations will arise that require you to reassess these ethics before making decisions.

Finance

It is never easy to 'make ends meet' when running a gymnastics club. Finance is always a problem. There are many ways in which a coach can increase income at the expense of the safety of the gymnast, but they are usually neither desirable nor advisable. For example, instead of having coach: gymnast ratios of say 1:6 in the club, this can be increased to 1:20. There is still only one coach being paid, but there is a greater revenue from more gymnasts. However, the safety and quality of coaching has been downgraded for the sake of finance. Only in very disciplined situations should large ratios be used; it is not recommended for beginners.

Similarly, when equipment starts to wear out and needs to be refurbished or replaced, the coach has the option of using inferior material, replacing with a cheaper model or delaying everything until the last minute. Any of these options may or may not turn out to be a false economy. To avoid potential dangers, you must decide which level your top gymnasts are working at and replace the equipment to facilitate that level.

There are times, too, when a gymnast must travel great distances to get to a competition. This can mean leaving in the early hours of the morning or arranging hotel accommodation for the night before. Hotel accommodation is better for the gymnast, but will be more expensive for the club.

The heating, and to some extent the lighting, in the gym can have a bearing on the number of injuries sustained. The ideal training hall should be kept to 19 to 21°C with lighting at approximately 1000 lux. It is expensive to keep the gym up to these standards and a financial decision may have to be made. Safety must come first, and lighting and heating must be of the right level. So the decision that has to be made might be to increase the number of gymnasts per hour, or cut the amount of time in the gym.

All these situations pose a direct finance-versus-safety question. The coach may have the final word, but generally it is left to others, with finance very often being the winner.

Sponsorship

It is very nice to have a competition sponsored by particular companies. There is normally a great deal of discussion concerning how much the sponsors are willing to give and what they want in return. They may require a 'photocall' at some unsuitable hour, or insist on certain apparel being worn which does not suit the gymnast. At the end of competitions some sponsors may require the gymnasts to sign autographs for an hour or so. Great demands are made of gymnasts, and the coach must decide whether to co-operate fully with the sponsors and keep them happy, or to be more selfish and only consider the well-being of the gymnasts and their preparation for the competition. It is a difficult decision and one which should be pointed out to the sponsors; then when the gymnasts refuse certain requests the sponsors may understand.

Political pressures

Within sport the word politics is a dirty word. Gymnastics is no different from any other sport. There are political pressures on the judge whether he/she is working at club, regional, national or international level. The higher the stakes, the greater the politics.

For a judge to be as impartial as possible he/she should ideally have no alliance with any gymnast or club; but though this is desirable, it is rarely the case. It is never the case when two nations come together for an International or compete in a major competition such as the World Championships. The temptation is to give just a few tenths extra to help the gymnast on her way; or maybe the judges' scruples are such that they refuse to allow themselves to give extra marks and in so doing can actually penalise the gymnast by being too harsh on her.

International goals

There are times when a gymnast reaches international level and has certain personal goals. However, her club, regional or national governing body may have ruled that a certain policy will be in force and certain allocations of resources may have been made. The two sides may well not agree. The gymnast and her coach must then ethically decide whether to 'go it alone' or to fulfil the wishes of the governing body. In most cases, it is better to work with the governing body and try to change the decision if possible.

Appointing and assessing coaches

The success of a strong gymnastics club is based on high-quality coaching. For a club to get the right coach, certain questions need to be taken into account. These include a detailed consideration of the coach's 'track record', how much time he/she can make available to the club, coaching qualifications, experience, availability to travel, other qualifications that have a bearing on gymnastics (such as first aid), payment required, and so on.

It is also a good plan to have a regular assessment of the work of coaching staff, though this poses the problem of confidentiality and must be carefully carried out. Remember that the Data Protection Act must be observed if the club uses any electronic storage medium.

Scientific research

Gymnastics lends itself very well to scientific research in various areas:

Mechanics. It is very easy to show mechanical principles using gymnasts as demonstrators.

Physiology. The female gymnast usually begins her career as a pre-pubescent child. Much research work is being carried out in to the 'training of young athletes' and it will be several years before any conclusions can be drawn from the findings. As the gymnast develops into maturity there can be an immense difference in the performance levels of the post-pubescent adult. Many physiological studies have been made and a know-ledge of strength, flexibility and cardiovascular norms are necessary to improve our understanding of the gymnast's performance.

Nutrition. The gymnast must look the part; gymnastics is an aesthetic sport. It is difficult for the gymnast to stay lean and to keep up the energy requirements necessary to performance at high level. Much research is needed to help gymnasts in this area.

Psychology. Gymnastics is about the mind as well as the body. Raw strength by itself will not win the day. For the psychologist to have an effect on the gymnast, time must be spent on psychological skills, and therefore time must be taken away from physical skills. Both are important and will play different roles at different times throughout the season.

Although it is agreed that all these areas of research can be beneficial, care must be taken to ensure that any course followed is not allowed to impinge too much on the privacy of the individual. The serious scientist must be allowed to research, but a delicate balance needs to be maintained so that the cost in terms of the limited training time of the gymnast is not too high. The sport must progress, but at what expense to our existing gymnasts?

Fair competition – drug testing

At present, in the sport of gymnastics, there is no known drug which will enhance performance. Even so, the authorities rightly drug-test competitors at random at major competitions; and it can be argued that ethically it is unfair to submit certain gymnasts to the pressure of what could be a traumatic experience for them.

Drug tests are done at random at the end of the round, after the gymnast has completed her competition. But just the thought of this experience may affect the performance of the gymnast, especially if she is as young as thirteen years old.

Pressure to compete

There are times in the year when a gymnast needs a psychological rest. There are also times when she needs a physical rest. Both of these are due to exhaustion, mainly through a long competition season. Sometimes gymnasts are injured and need time to recover. Is it ethical for the teacher or coach to put pressure on the gymnast by asking her to represent her club, region or country at such a time? She could do it, but would the cost be too high? Maybe it is the mental well-being of the gymnast which is at risk, and if so, again at what cost? The coach must seriously consider his/her own motives before deciding what to do.

Technical competence

Coaches wish to do the best they can for each individual gymnast and to maximise their potential at all times. To do this they need to go on many courses, which takes up a great deal of time – time that could have been spent in the gym. But there must be a balance between working in the gym with the gymnasts and going on courses. Not enough courses could damage the gymnasts' potential; too many could have the same result.

Social relationships

The gymnastics club has a social responsibility. It is regarded as part of the community. Classes can start at under five years of age and develop through to competitive and recreational levels. The coach has a very special relationship with the children. They are not forced to go to the gym, and so it is the atmosphere the coach creates that makes them want to go back again. If not, they would soon leave and join a club that did satisfy them. The coach must run the club with discipline due to the nature of the sport, but through this discipline the gymnast must be able to see care and success. Once gymnast and coach have respect for each other a long and fruitful relationship will follow. As a coach, you must be aware that you are dealing with girls at a very impressionable age, and you need to take into account the parents' wishes and the way they want their children to grow up. Teenage girls tend to look for guidance from an outsider, and this could well be you.

In conclusion, it must be recognised that the gymnastics club, coaches, parents, administrators and gymnasts are all part of the community. Decisions made within the club could affect many people in the community, and the ethics of whether this or that decision is the right one will be endlessly debated. However, the decisions that most people will accept are those which give priority to the safety and well-being of young children. If decisions are made keeping these things in mind, then at least we shall have happy, safe gymnasts.

10 Preparing teams for competitions

In an ideal world the teacher or coach will have selected the team well in advance of the competition and all the physical and psychological preparations will have been done. Even so there are still a number of things to take into account.

Tactics

The team should be selected on scores and reliability if the goal is to win the team event. In a World Championships, six gymnasts make up a team and the highest five scores count on each piece of apparatus. The coach must check the competition rules and select the team accordingly. Not every team event is run along the same lines as a World Championships. A gymnast might be selected for a team who would stand a good chance of an individual final or would boost the team score on say two or three pieces; if she counted on any other piece then this would be a bonus.

International rules are set for major competitions and these are adhered to rigorously. Local competitions may have slightly different rules. Your tactics may have to vary accordingly.

Surprises

Surprises are things which you should try to avoid around competition time. They are variables which are outside your control. The build-up to a competition starts some hours before and it is important to get the gymnasts in the right frame of mind. Surprises can ruin this build-up and affect their concentration.

Travelling

If the team is to travel by bus, train, ferry or anything that runs to a timetable, make sure that you all meet with plenty of time to spare. It has been known for such types of transport to leave early or not run at all. Panic then begins to set in. Alternative travel arrangements are made in a hurry, arrival at the venue is late, the team has lost the allocated warm-up slot. All of these things have happened before and will happen again. They are not good for any gymnast, especially inexperienced ones. This kind of thing is not conducive to good performances. Arrive in plenty of time!

On arrival

On arriving at the competition site, look for a telephone just in case an accident occurs and an ambulance is needed in a hurry. Check that ice is available, or the nearest substitute for ice. If it is possible, take your own ice in an ice box. It will stay frozen for at least six hours. At all BAGA national competitions medical assistance is required to be available in the arena at all times. Try to find out what experience the medical team have of gymnastics, and make yourself known to them. It is useful to have met with a person beforehand if you need their services in an emergency.

Temperature

It is desirable to compete in a hall which is comfortably warm, about 20°C. This is not always the case and therefore the gymnasts should come suitably clothed for the occasion. It is easy to discard clothing if it isn't needed, much more difficult to find some. Many thin woollen layers are desirable; they will trap warm air between each layer. Salopettes in the winter are ideal for moving between the competition pieces and also from home to the venue. A hat is excellent for warmth; gloves should also not be forgotten.

Team spirit

A team should be unified. Many gymnasts can find added strength when working for a team. Make sure the members of the team can identify with each other. Try to get track suits, shoes, socks, ribbons etc. all matching. Leotards *must* be identical; this is a rule. They must fit well and be comfortable. The gymnasts must feel good in them if they are going to perform well.

Try to let the other teams see that your team is confident and well prepared. There are many ways of doing this. You might use a well choreographed team warm-up to prepared music. When the gymnasts march to each piece, make sure they accentuate the steps, nothing half-hearted. When they arrive at their next piece, have them stand and present in front of the head judge. Let everyone know they mean business!

Parents

Her parents are the most important and influential people to the gymnast in everything she does, so much so that they can be a great motivator to the gymnast and a considerable support in competitions. But beware, they can also destroy a gymnast before they have even set foot in the arena. It is a good idea for the coach to have a few quiet words with the gymnast to see how she feels about her parents at competitions. If it is too much for her to cope with, then the parents should be told. Situations have occurred whereby parents secretly sneak in to watch their child and then rush out afterwards so that the child does not know and doesn't have to handle any extra pressure. However, care must be taken, since this can open a whole new 'can of worms' if the child finds out.

It may be necessary politely to remove certain parents from the competition arena. Problems can arise in the following situations:

- Parents can destroy the child's confidence just by turning up to support her.
- The child can *think* that the parents' expectations of her are too high and worry about it so much that she performs badly.
- The parents' expectations of the gymnast *are* too high.
- Parents embarrass the child by clapping too vigorously, or shouting encouragement.
- They try to motivate the child by using negative comments.
- They boo at rival performances.
- They heckle the judge for unfavourable scores.
- They try to attract the child's attention instead of letting her build up her concentration for her next performance.
- The gymnast may know that the parents have sacrificed something in order to be there to watch her, and this may have a negative effect.

Know the gymnasts

During the competition you need to know how each gymnast likes to prepare herself for the next performance she is going to give. Some like to be very active and practise some of the elements. Others prefer to sit, close their eyes and psychologically perform the whole routine perfectly. Some gymnasts think that they should be active when probably they should be doing some mental practice, or vice-versa. It takes an experienced coach to recognise that a change is necessary in a gymnast's preparation for an exercise, and implement it successfully.

On some occasions a gymnast will give a very poor performance, present herself to the judges and storm off towards the team, throwing tantrums, crying, saying how unfair it was, etc. Everything will be negative – all the statements that the rest of the team do not want to hear before they compete. On such an occasion it is prudent to separate this gymnast from the rest until she has regained her composure and starts thinking of the team again and not just about herself.

Praise

Gymnasts look to the teacher or coach for an appraisal of their performance. There is no point in lying, but the 'sandwich' approach to criticism should be considered. Start off with a positive comment, then put in the criticism and finish off with another positive comment. Gymnasts do not respect someone who is not truthful with them. They already know whether or not the performance was good. It is really confirmation of that, as much as anything else, which they are looking for.

Behavioural patterns

Gymnasts can be like Jekyll and Hyde in personality as they go through a competition. You must recognise their different moods and try to channel them towards a good performance. Body language is important. Gymnasts, more than most sports people, can tell you a great deal without saying a word. Watch how they move when they walk into the competition, how they warm up, nervous habits before a big move, how the body reacts after a good or bad routine. If you pick up these signs early enough, you can sometimes alleviate a problem or encourage some positive actions.

Stress

The competition arena is full of stress. The competitors, coaches, judges, organisers, scorers, TV producers and so on all react differently and show their stress in different ways. Before the competition they can be very nice, easygoing, lovable people, but during the competition their whole character may well change. If the change is for the worse, stay away; but if it is for the better try to capitalise on it.

   As well as trying to perform the practical aspect of the job, the teacher or coach must try to reduce stress for him/herself and the gymnasts so that they can perform to their potential. Keep the gymnasts working as a unit and try to keep their attention away from officials. It has been known for coaches to make incorrect decisions after getting flustered or annoyed by some official.

Conclusion

Taking a team of gymnasts around a competition can be likened to a game of chess. There are so many variables, some under your control and some not, but all of them playing their part. It takes a long time to become a good coach of a team and many mistakes will be made along the way. There is no formula which will work with every team but eventually you will find a set of rules or guidelines which will work for most of the time. The requirements you need to be a good coach to one team are the same as those required to be a good coach to any team; but there is no substitute for experience.

Park Ji Sook, Korea

11 Managing sports injuries

Gymnastics is a sport where the body is continually turning upside down and creating many different shapes. The gymnast's spatial and kinaesthetic awareness sometimes lets her down and an injury occurs. On other occasions it is just the rigour of the sport which takes its toll and causes injury. Gymnastics injuries fall into various categories:

- First aid
- Minor injury
- Soft tissue injury
- Fracture
- Head and spinal injury
- Over-use injury
- Growth-related injury

There are professional people available who can help minimise the recovery period. In some instances they may even be able to prevent the injury from occurring. These people should be consulted whenever possible.

When an injury occurs, the initial treatment is very important. If the right person administers it at the right time the recovery time to full fitness will be as short as possible. Education plays a large part in this. The rigours of gymnastics are as individual as any other sport. Even the professionals (doctors, physiotherapists and so on) will need some education before they can use their expertise.

The teacher or coach has certain responsibilities and is the key to managing sports injuries. It is your job to decide which direction to take, whom to see, when and why. It is also your job to educate the professionals to the needs of gymnasts. If the right principles are followed a quick recovery time will result.

First aid

In a gymnasium full of young children it is the teacher or coach who is responsible for first aid. There is a basic level at which you must be knowledgeable and which you must be capable of administering before the experts take over.

Consider first the most extreme case: there can be many reasons why a sporting person could stop breathing and their heart stop beating. In this situation it is the coach in the gym who has to take action. There is approximately four minutes before brain damage occurs due to oxygen starvation. Assessment of the situation and action must be taken in this time. You should know where the nearest telephone is situated as an ambulance will be necessary. You should be aware of the adults who are present and which of them, if any, have qualifications or experience with situations like this. It is advisable for you to know the techniques of mouth-to-mouth resuscitation and how to restart a heart should this be necessary. There are few situations where time is of the essence, but this is one of them.

A punctured artery could be another such situation. With little knowledge, panic can set in and incorrect decisions be made. A simple sterile wad placed over the area and pressure applied is all that is necessary until medical help arrives. If that particular part of the body can be higher than the heart, so much the better.

The most common injuries in gymnastics tend to be damage to soft tissue or bone. The initial treatment of these is the same. In determining the action to be taken the following things need to be assessed:

- Which piece of apparatus was involved?
- Did she land on the apparatus?
- How did she hit the floor?
- Was there sudden pain? Sometimes it subsides and numbness takes over for 20 – 30 minutes.

On inspection of the injury:

- Was there any deformity?
- Was there rapid swelling?
- Was there point tenderness, especially over bony parts?
- Was there indirect tenderness, i.e. can pain be felt at the injured site if another part of the limb is moved?
- Can a grating sound be heard at the injury site?
- Is there more movement than normal at the injury site, as though there might be an extra joint there?
- Is there discoloration? (This sometimes does not happen for a few days.)

If there is any suspicion of a fracture, medical advice should be sought immediately and the injured part should not be moved.

Rest, ice, compression and elevation should follow unless there is a compound (open) fracture. Talking to medical people seems to indicate some discrepancy as to the length of time for which ice should be applied to the injured area. When ice is first applied, the blood vessels contract, restricting the blood flow, which is highly desirable. But after a while the area gets so cold that the blood vessels dilate to bring blood and warmth back to the area, and this is very undesirable. Each medical person has his own preference but it would seem reasonable to ice the injured area for up to 5 minutes, reassess the injury and then intermittently ice the injured area for up to 15–20 minutes. The overall length of time over which ice is applied may well depend upon the depth of the injury.

When icing is finished, the compression bandage can be left on to alleviate any further possible swelling. The gymnast should not bear weight on the injured part and, if in doubt, should be taken to a medical person for a professional diagnosis.

The next 24–48 hours should see a continuation of cooling to relieve the swelling and the pain. The compression bandage can be replaced by a support bandage and there should be continued rest. Elevation and no weight loading of the injured part is still important. After 48 hours the injury should be beginning to resolve and the gymnast can be gradually rehabilitated back to full training. This process may require the help of medical personnel.

Foam pits

A gymnast is one of the few athletes who trains in a gymnasium which uses foam pits. These pits create their own safety problems. It is not uncommon for an injury to occur in a pit when one part of the body sticks in the foam whilst the rest of the body continues to move. Twists of the knee, ankle and spine are most common. If this happens then you should make sure that the gymnast is instructed not to move, and the most experienced person present who can deal with the situation should ease themselves into the pit to assess the damage. In most cases the easiest way of getting the injured person out of the pit is on a stiff mat.

A course in first aid with the St John Ambulance Brigade or the Red Cross is advisable. This kind of information is essential to the coach. One day you might just have to apply it.

Minor injury

Gymnastics is no different from any other sport and gymnasts will pick up their fair share of minor injuries. The cut finger, grazed knee, irritation in the eye, nose bleed, splinters from a wooden floor are but a few which could need attention. This type of injury and the treatment of it is dealt with quite adequately in the first aid manuals of the St John Ambulance Brigade and the Red Cross.

Soft tissue injury

This relates to muscle, tendon or ligament injury. It can vary in severity from, for example, a minor muscle pull or sprained ligament to a complete tendon rupture or joint dislocation. After the necessary period of rest it is important that, when all pain and swelling has gone, the full range of joint movement is restored and any wasting of the muscle is rectified before the gymnast is allowed back into full training.

Physiotherapists may be involved with this process, using one or more machines, mobilisation techniques and a suitable exercise programme.

Fracture

If the coach suspects that a gymnast has broken a bone it can only be confirmed by X-ray. It would be prudent to refer the gymnast to the hospital. The most likely treatment would be immobilisation, and a suitable rehabilitation programme will need to be followed once the fracture has healed. This is likely to follow the same procedure as for soft tissue injury.

Head and spinal injury

It is possible for a gymnast to receive a blow to the head but have no after-effects other than a swelling. Caution should be exercised in case of delayed effects, and the gymnast should be made to sit down for a reasonable period. Any abnormal behaviour resulting from an event occurring during training should be reported to the parents and possibly referred to a physician.

There are occasions when the gymnast lands awkwardly on her neck or back. In this situation, initially treat the gymnast for a suspected broken spine. Assuming there is no external danger, e.g. fire, she should be left where she is and an ambulance called, stressing the nature of the injury. The paramedic will examine her and then arrange the transfer to a hospital. He/she will make sure that the following procedure is carried out.

The gymnast should be fitted with a collar to restrict involuntary movements of the head. Any torque can cause spinal damage or nerve root damage when small fractures are present. She should be transported on a spinal stretcher. One individual should be given the responsibility of maintaining the alignment of the head and neck with the long axis of the body.

If later it is found that a break has not occurred, then no harm has been done.

Over-use injuries

Gymnasts are prone to micro-trauma in the muscles, bones and joints because of the repetitive nature of training. It can also be caused by poor technique or poor conditioning. An example is the damage caused to the front of the ankle by repetitive short landings from backward saltos. In this situation the gymnast is leaning forwards when she makes contact with the floor. Eventually this causes very small fractures due to the repeated knocking together of the ankle bone (talus) and the shin bone (tibia). These small bony deposits can cause inflammation in the joint capsule and tendon sheaths. Over the years the body lays down new bone to protect itself. This in itself causes problems to the range of flexion of the joint, and so the condition is self-perpetuating.

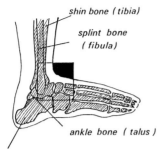

shin bone (tibia)

splint bone
(fibula)

ankle bone (talus)

heel bone (calcaneus)

Treatment for this is to strengthen and mobilise the joint. In severe cases an orthopaedic specialist may administer a cortisone injection or operate to pare down the build-up of bone. In some cases this spur of bone breaks off into the joint and an operation is then necessary to remove it.

Prevention is the best cure in all cases, and so it would be prudent to make sure that as many soft landings as possible are made available to the gymnast. Only when she is getting close to a competition should she come out of soft landing surfaces and prepare the proprioceptors of the ankle for the firmer landing surfaces.

It is inevitable that at some stage a gymnast will land short, and a good conditioning programme will help in any one-off situation. If a gymnast is continually landing short, it is advisable for her to stay away from firm landing surfaces until the skill has been perfected. Competition is a powerful motivator, but if it is likely to produce a short landing then prudence and time should prevail: there is always tomorrow!

Stress fractures

If a bone is repeatedly stressed it may eventually lead to a stress fracture. In women's gymnastics the most common site for a stress fracture is on the fibula bone, about 5 cm up from the lateral malleolus. This can be caused through road running in poor training shoes or repeated jumping and landing in the gym. Pain will initially occur when the gymnast is working in the gym. There will be no apparent reason for the pain which will typically have developed over 6–8 weeks. When training is finished the pain fades. The gymnast will then begin to experience pain during training and a dull ache after training. There will be tenderness and perhaps swelling over the area. Given the symptoms outlined, the coach should consider the possibility of a stress fracture and direct the gymnast to consult an orthopaedic specialist. Rehabilitation of 6–12 weeks should remedy the problem.

Growth-related injury

There are a few injuries that keep re-occurring in every sport and the symptoms should be recognised. In childhood and adolescence respect must be shown to the growing skeletal system. All the jumping gymnasts do can result in injuries where the muscle attaches to the bone. When the muscle contracts, it causes the tendon to start pulling at its insertion to the bone. This is most common at two major sites: where the quadriceps muscles attach to the tibia, just below the kneecap (tibial tuberosity), and where the Achilles tendon attaches to the heel bone (calcaneus). These are known as Osgood-Schlatters Disease and Severs Disease respectively. In early stages of the disease the painful area should be rested and ice could be applied. In severe cases gymnasts have been put into plaster for 2–6 weeks, during which time the condition generally settles down. Eventually, after puberty, ossification, caused by the laying down of extra bone at the two sites mentioned, will result in a small lump.

Preventing injury

Prevention is the best cure for injury. Many people in regular contact with the gymnast can help prevent injury, and there are others who should be made available to her from time to time.

Parents

The parents of a gymnast will need to learn how to feed their child the correct nutritional food for her particular sport. The diet for a marathon runner is very different from that of a gymnast, and so on. The correct food will fuel the gymnast for the type of activity she is expected to carry out. The wrong food could result in early exhaustion and fatigue, possibly resulting in an injury. It is also the parents' responsibility to ensure that their child attends to her injuries conscientiously, and generally to inspire confidence and provide moral support.

Physiologists

It is useful to ask a physiologist to screen the gymnast, both before she takes up the sport and at regular intervals thereafter. He/she can analyse the condition of the heart and lungs and determine if they are appropriately conditioned for what the training is asking of them.

The spine needs to be inspected to see if it has any defects; if it does, the coach needs to recognise them and select work that avoids that weakness. The gymnast should be given advice on how to correct the defect.

The balance of the skeletal muscles needs to be checked. The muscles of the left side of the body should be equal to those of the right. If the biceps of the upper arm have been developed, then so too should the triceps (agonist, antagonist). Any imbalance can lead to injury.

At different stages of a child's growth the long bones of the body can be unequal in length. During adolescence there may also be great changes in body shape, e.g. height, weight, distribution of muscle mass, strength, speed, etc. When this occurs it takes time for the gymnast to re-educate her body for balance and co-ordination. At times like this it may be useful to consolidate work rather than push forward with new work.

Height and weight are closely related. If this ratio changes so that the gymnast becomes very heavy for her height then her work will become very sluggish and injury may well occur. Puberty can be the cause of this and it can be traumatic for the gymnast. It can be just as traumatic for the coach!

Many physiological changes occur at puberty, and these should be monitored. If the coach is aware of these changes, this can be a happy and safe period for the gymnast. With added weight and a new shape the gymnast has to change and modify her timing on the apparatus. She must work harder and faster to achieve the same results.

Doctors

It is often not understood that in their training general practitioners only spend a very small amount of time on injury and rehabilitation. Even less time, if any, is spent on the sport of gymnastics in particular. It is worth finding a doctor who has worked with sports injuries and understands the physical requirements of gymnastics. He/she will be able to use such skills to greater effect and return the gymnast to training in the least amount of time and more safely.

Physiotherapists

Most chartered physiotherapists work in hospitals and clinics and never see a gymnastics hall, so they need to learn about the amount and type of forces required in gymnastics. If at all possible, encourage them to attend a gym and let them see the gymnast taking off, landing, rolling, working asymmetric bars, etc. Without this knowledge on the part of the physiotherapist, it is possible that an injured gymnast who has followed a rehabilitation programme will start training again too early.

The gymnast herself

The general age of female gymnasts can be anything up to their early twenties. In that time they will possibly be injured at least once. Sometimes the injury is obvious but at other times the pain just appears over a period of time. The gymnast must be encouraged to keep a dialogue going with her teacher or coach, telling him or her how she is feeling on each day of training. Has she had a hard physical day at school, or does she feel exhausted after yesterday's training? Has she just finished examinations at school, has she just started a period, has she just been on a school trip and spent the last two hours on a bus? All of these situations have a bearing on how the gymnast is going to perform in the gym that evening.

In the gym she might get a niggle of pain from a certain activity. She should be encouraged to tell you, so that you can note it in her training book in case it develops at a later stage. At least you will then know which move aggravated the injury and can guard against it.

Teachers and Coaches

Everything that affects the gymnast whilst in the gym must also concern her teacher or coach. If the gymnast is not forthcoming with information, then you must ask the questions. At the beginning of the training session, enquire about her health. Does she have any new injuries or are the old ones any worse? Did she follow instructions and see the doctor or physiotherapist or have an X-ray as requested? You need to be able to read the gymnast's body language. Look to see if she is walking properly, if the handstands are straight, if she is holding her wrist or back, if she is wriggling her head about in an unusual way. All of these things are an unconscious indication from the gymnast that something is not quite right.

It is worth talking to parents to see if they have noticed any changes in their children. Sometimes the gymnast does need help but is too afraid or shy to speak directly, and the parents need to be her mouthpiece.

Injuries can occur if the gymnast does not carry out a good warm-up. In warm temperatures (23–25°C), a 20-minute warm-up might suffice. In colder conditions (15–20°C) the warm-up might need to be extended to 30 minutes. It is your responsibility to make sure that the warm-up is done thoroughly.

Sport psychologists

A good sport psychologist can help in training. There are many mental skills which can be taught so as to alleviate certain situations both in the gym and at competitions. For this to be effective, the psychologist will need to visit the gym to learn the pressures and requirements of the sport before he/she can offer advice and use his/her skills to the full.

Conclusion

For a gymnast to stay fit for the majority of her career is an art. Some injuries are pure accidents and cannot be foreseen. But if the right people are involved and do their jobs correctly then injuries should be minimal.

When an injury occurs the correct first aid will reduce the amount of time during which gymnasts have to stay away from the gym; so it is important that trained people are on hand to administer this treatment.

Choose doctors and chartered physiotherapists carefully. Finding the right people with the right skills and with a working knowledge of the sport will get the gymnast back into the gym in the shortest, safest time possible.

As teacher or coach you must make sure that you have a network of professionals around you that you can call upon when necessary.

Part II
The skills

12 The vault

Handspring vault

The key to all good-quality vaulting is the handspring vault. It is the most basic of the overswing vaults and needs to be taught carefully. The only type of vault which does not relate very well to the handspring is the round-off family of vaults.

The handspring vault can be considered in seven phases: (1) the approach run, (2) the hurdle step, (3) the springboard take-off, (4) the first flight, (5) the thrust, (6) the second flight and (7) the landing.

1 The approach run

The gymnast's approach run should be measured, either from the middle of the horse or from the leading edge of the horse, to a precise distance agreed by coach and gymnast. It is not a good idea to measure from the leg of the horse as the position of the legs will vary in different styles of vaulting horse – some do not even have four legs! The gymnast should stand at the agreed position either with both feet together ready to take a step, or already in the running position with one foot in front of the other. No shuffling around of the feet is acceptable. She should accelerate towards the horse in the same way as a sprinter in athletics, with the aim of achieving maximum controllable speed before the hurdle step. The arms should be bent to 90° at the elbow, moving parallel to each other, with the hands and shoulders relaxed. It is quite common, but inefficient, to see the shoulders hunched and the arms straight or crossing in front of the body. These actions introduce unnecessary tensions in the body and disrupt the smooth rhythm of the correct running style; they should be discouraged. The legs should also move parallel to each other, with a good lift of the knee each time. Another common fault is for the gymnast to flick her heels up behind her without lifting her knees. If the distance has been measured accurately, and if the run-up has been practised sufficiently, no adjustment should be necessary. The gymnast will be able to run smoothly and with confidence to an exact stride pattern, concentrating fully on the vault to be performed.

Lavinia Agache, Romania

As the gymnast grows and gets stronger and faster, her running style will change. The run-up should be checked periodically, and modified to allow for these changes.

2 The hurdle step

The last step of the run should be flat-footed to allow the gymnast to change direction and move onto the springboard. Whilst this is happening the arms should gather just behind the hips, ready to swing forward and upwards in an arc whilst the feet are in contact with the board. This technique has an advantage for small, light gymnasts because the underarm swing will cause the springboard to depress a little further. This added force can aid height and/or rotation.

During the hurdle step the feet move in front of the shoulders to contact the board. The position of the shoulders in relation to the feet will help determine the height and rotation of the first flight.

The physiological make up of the gymnast will determine the speed and angle at which she leaves the board. If the gymnast has predominantly fast muscle twitch fibres which contract quickly, then her approach speed will be high. The ability of the muscles to contract quickly will enable the gymnast to get on and off the springboard quickly, and on and off the horse quickly. There will still be a compression time on the springboard and horse but it will be relatively short. (Compression time is the time it takes for the springboard/horse/gymnast to change shape, due to the forces acting upon them, before the gymnast moves off in the intended direction at an intended speed.) Gymnasts who have slower reactions, due to their slower muscle twitch fibres, may have to change their angles onto the springboard and horse to allow for the longer time they spend in contact with the apparatus.

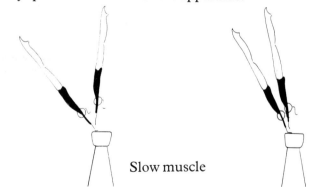

Slow muscle   Fast muscle

Body compression time when hitting the apparatus

3 The springboard take-off

When the gymnast strikes the springboard, one of her first aims is to reach the horse in the shortest possible time so that horizontal deceleration is minimised. Her second aim is to strike the horse in the desired shape and her third is to strike the horse at an angle which will achieve a high second flight (or post-flight) with enough rotation to land without making corrections. Realisation of these aims is dependent on the distance of the springboard from the horse, the speed and angle at which the gymnast strikes the springboard and her reaction times when in contact with the apparatus.

The gymnast needs to maintain forward velocity when she strikes the springboard. In order to achieve this the shoulders should not be too far behind the feet when she strikes the springboard. There is a compression phase of the body on the board and during this time the gymnast changes body shape to leave the springboard in the first or pre-flight phase. The physical height of the gymnast will determine her entry angle on to the springboard in order to achieve the correct take-off position. Smaller gymnasts may need to be more upright when they leave the springboard, taller ones may need to lean forward more. All gymnasts should retain good body tension to maximise the effectiveness of the board contact phase, thus producing adequate height and rotation.

4   The first flight

The shape of the body through the air should be very slightly 'dished', with the arms in line with the head, and no apparent shoulder angle.

5   The thrust

When the gymnast makes contact with the horse she should be at an angle which will allow compression to take place but still allow her to leave the horse before the body's CG passes the vertical. The shape of the body when it initially makes contact should be very slightly 'dished'. This 'dish' should then stretch out and the gymnast should leave the horse in a slight arch. To the untrained eye the body will look as though it has remained straight throughout the thrust phase. The head should remain in a neutral position during contact with the horse, so that the gymnast can just see her hands.

The top of the horse can be regarded as a launching platform. If the gymnast leaves the horse well before the vertical, the parabolic flight path will be high and short (A). If she were to leave on the vertical there would be a better balance between height and length (B). A late release from the horse would result in the gymnast getting little height but more length (C).

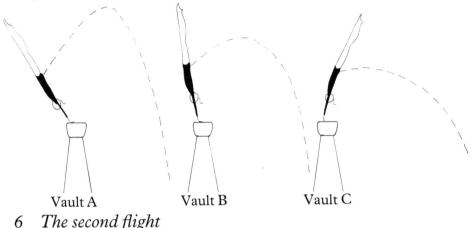

Vault A   Vault B   Vault C

6 The second flight

As the gymnast leaves the horse, her head should rotate forward slightly so that she can see her feet and spatially orientate herself for the landing. The body should be kept in a straight line with the arms over the head. If the gymnast does not have enough rotation to land correctly then she can (a) lower the arms and (b) create a 'dish' down the length of the body. Both these actions shorten the body and will thus increase her rate of rotation. Furthermore, if the gymnast lowers her arms backwards her body will tilt forwards.

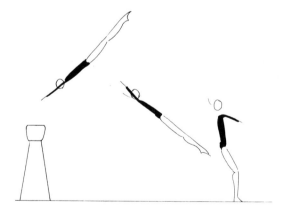

7 The landing

Just before landing the gymnast should begin to lower her arms to the side to improve stability of the landing. The landing of all vaults should take as long as possible, in order to reduce the size of the forces acting on the body. To achieve this the gymnast contacts the floor fully stretched, and then sequentially flexes the joints starting at the toes. This gives each joint muscle group the opportunity to play its part as shock absorber. The spine will also absorb some forces between each vertebra, and care should be taken to ensure that the back is straight during landing (and other thrust phases) so that the risk of injury is minimised.

Mechanics of the move

During the run-up the gymnast drives each leg downwards and backwards into the floor with a certain force. It is the simultaneous ground reaction force, acting forwards and upwards, that drives the gymnast forwards (Newton's Third Law of Motion). When the gymnast hits the board she again applies a force, this time to the springboard. The diagram below shows the reaction to this force broken down into its vertical and horizontal components. The resultant force (Fr) is eccentric, i.e. it does not pass through the centre of gravity (CG) of the body, and therefore it creates rotation.

An additional force may be applied by the armswing. If the gymnast were to raise her arms whilst in the air, her body and legs would move downwards. If she were to repeat this arm action whilst in contact with the board, the same tendency of the body and legs to move downwards would result in a force being applied to the springboard. There must also be a simultaneous reaction force exerted by the springboard on the gymnast. This 'armswing reaction force' can be added to those forces generated by the gymnast jumping on the board, thereby increasing the resultant force acting on the gymnast.

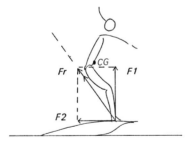

Reaction forces (F1 and F2)
Resultant force (Fr)

The underswing action of the arms going forwards and upwards will also cause the body to tilt further forwards, thus assisting forward rotation.

When the gymnast makes contact with the horse, she applies forces to it. The reaction force can again be seen in its vertical and horizontal components. The resultant force (Fr) does not go through the CG of the body and therefore rotation occurs.

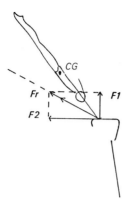

During the first and second flight the gymnast's CG must follow a parabolic curve. She can change shape and thereby redistribute her mass around the CG, but the CG has to follow mechanical laws and cannot change the parabolic curve until the ground is reached.

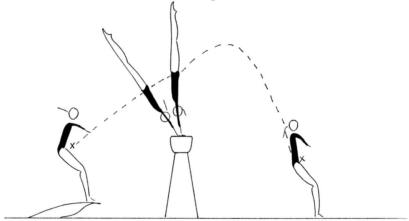

Progressions

Key points

- Run-up should be fast.
- Rotation from the board should be rapid.
- There should be strong shoulder repulsion from the horse.
- The gymnast must leave the horse as or before she reaches the vertical.
- Tension must be maintained throughout the vault.

1. The gymnast should kick to handstand vigorously and try to hop on the hands. If she can do this, then she should try to hop up a small step.

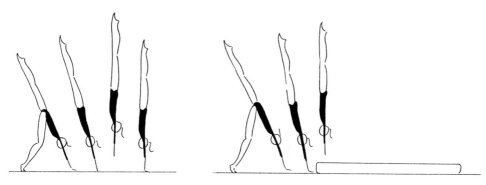

2. Have the gymnast do straight saltos from a trampette and then from a springboard. She must *think* of leading with the heels throughout the practice.

3. Landing practices are important. They should start from different heights without rotation and then add the rotation.

4. The practice shown below should be done to orientate the gymnast to thrust and rotate. At the same time the release shape can be learned.

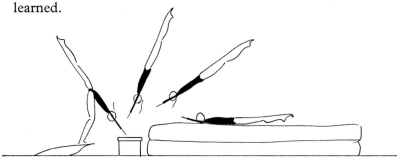

5. Progression 4 can now be developed with a longer run and a two-footed take-off. The height of the horse can be taken up in stages.

6. If thrust and second flight need attention, a trampette could be introduced as a muscle replacer, enabling the gymnast to complete more repetitions without getting fatigued.

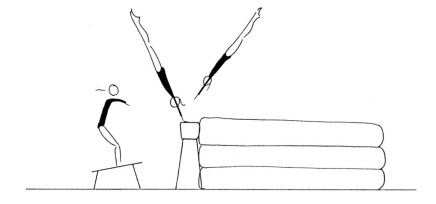

7.   If the gymnasts are very young and do not have the musculature to use a springboard for this vault, then a bench leading up to a trampette and padded vault would be useful.

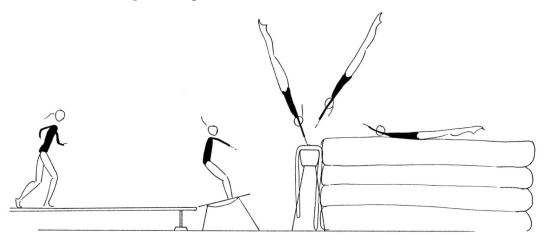

8.   A trampette and eventually a springboard can be used to practise the complete vault.

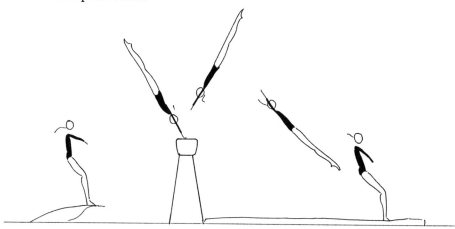

Specific conditioning

1.   Once strength has been developed in the legs, a slight inclined run of about 30 m long will help to accentuate the lean forward, drive the arms hard and make the knees lift.

2. As well as uphill running, downhill running (5° decline) will help the gymnast run a little faster than normal and can help to educate the muscle firings to occur together, or at least closer together, to maximise thrust over the shortest amount of time, thereby increasing speed.

3. Plyometrics (rebound jump work) can help board take-off, but this should only be done for short periods of time and with athletes who have already done some conditioning. Some pre-pubescent gymnasts can be prone to Severs Disease (tendon insertion pull) if they do too much of this work.

4. To prepare the gymnast for impact with the horse, some shoulder resistance work will be necessary. Support the gymnast in handstand and get her to sag and extend through the shoulder girdle. This must eventually be done very fast because this action on the horse happens very fast.

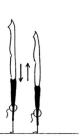
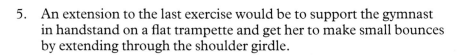

5. An extension to the last exercise would be to support the gymnast in handstand on a flat trampette and get her to make small bounces by extending through the shoulder girdle.

6. Repetitive squat jumps and jumps from a horse will help to control the landing phase of the vault.

Handspring vault with full twist

To be able to perform this vault with any degree of success, the gymnast must be able to perform a good handspring vault. When she has left the board her first flight should be slightly 'dished'. When she strikes the horse she extends through a straight line.

It is possible to initiate the twist with any combination of the three twisting techniques available, i.e. torque, cat or tilt. The most aesthetic comes from the tilt twist.

Tilt twist. The gymnast should leave the horse before she initiates the twist. When she is in the air she drops one straight arm sideways to the corresponding leg to initiate the twist. From the gymnast's viewpoint, if she dropped her right arm this would cause the body to turn anti-clockwise and vice-versa. It is important to lift the arm back above the head before landing to remove the tilt and stop the twist.

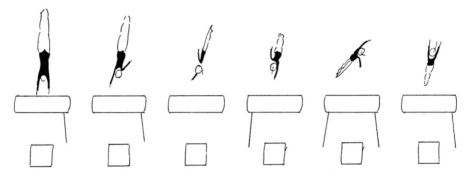

Torque/tilt. In reality pure tilt twisting rarely happens and a slight torque is set through the body even though in good vaults it cannot be detected easily. Having completed 90° of twist as a result of the torque created on the horse, the gymnast should initiate the tilt by dropping one arm forwards to her hips. In fact she may find it easier to tilt and then untilt herself by moving the arm in a circle, diagonally downwards and across the body to her left hip and then back upwards to its starting position.

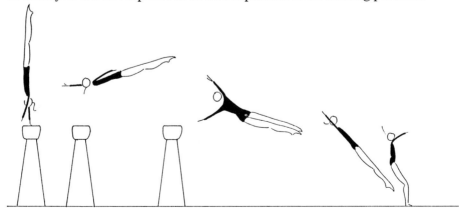

Mechanics of the move

The mechanics of the board take-off, first flight and thrust phases have already been covered in the description of the handspring vault.

Assuming from the gymnast's viewpoint that she wished to turn anti-clockwise, on leaving the horse she should drop her stretched right arm to her side. In reaction, the legs move to meet the arm, the result being a tilt to the left. As the gymnast is rotating forwards, she will twist anti-clockwise. If the gymnast maintained this position (right arm by side, left arm raised) until she landed she would still be leaning to the left, and would need to take a corrective step in that direction. It is therefore important for her to remove the tilt by raising the right arm or by lowering the left, as shown in the diagram on p. 101.

Progressions

Key points

- A sound handspring vault.
- The gymnast must leave the horse as or before she reaches the vertical.
- A strong arm action at the right time.

1. The gymnast forward rolls to back, lying with extended arms by the ears, shoulders and legs just off the floor.

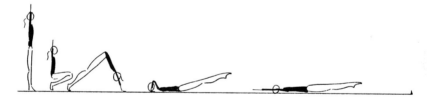

2. Same progression as 1, but as the gymnast gets to the finishing position she drops one arm (say the right arm) to the left hip.

Michaela Stanulet, Romania

3. As the gymnast gets to the finishing position in 2, ask her to roll to the left (anti-clockwise), trapping her right arm under her body.

4. As the gymnast gets to the finishing position in 3, ask her to roll again in the same direction, and at the same time raise her right hand to be equal and parallel to the left.

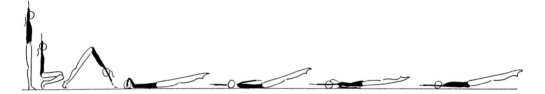

5. Using a box top and safety landing modules slightly higher than the box top, ask the gymnast to handspring from one leg to land on her back on the safety landing modules and then repeat progressions 1–4 on the landing modules.

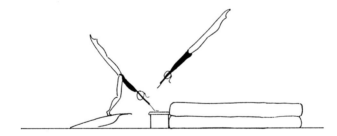

6. Using the same apparatus set up as for 5, now ask the gymnast to complete the arm drop before landing. Sometimes the half turn will occur, sometimes the gymnast will need to be told to spot the safety landing modules whilst the arm is being lowered to the opposite hip. 'Spotting' the safety modules enhances the torque created during contact with the horse.

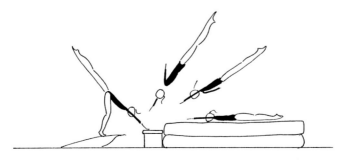

7. Follow the same practice as 6, and when the gymnast lands ask her to roll the next half of the turn and return the arm to its original position.

8. Have the gymnast attempt the complete full turn to land on her back on the safety landing modules. When attempts to do this are successful, the gymnast rarely lands square down the middle of the mat. This is because a little too much torque twist has been initiated from the box top too early and/or the tilt twist has not been untilted.

9. A run and first flight can now be added to this progression. A trampette can be used instead of a board to maximise skill and minimise effort. The landing side should have a platform or trampoline with a safety landing module on it to ensure the practice is safe.

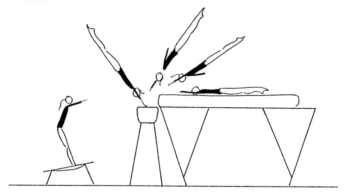

10. The whole vault can now be attempted, but still using the trampette.

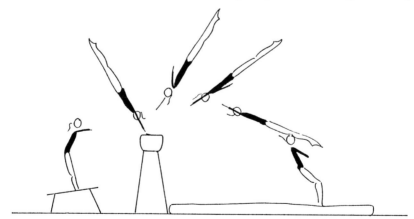

11. Once the skill has been learned a springboard can be substituted for the trampette and the complete vault can be attempted.

Specific conditioning

All the conditioning exercises for the handspring vault should be included.

1. An exercise for both orientation and conditioning would be to jump with a full turn from different heights. This would enable the gymnast to experience different speeds of twist and at the same time condition the legs for landing.

Tsukahara vault

The Tsukahara vault was named after the great Japanese gymnast of that name. From the basic tucked Tsukahara this move can progress to the pike, straight, half, full, one and a half and double twisting vaults. Very, very few gymnasts even consider doing a double back Tsukahara. To perform the Tsukahara correctly the gymnast should have a fast run-up. As she reaches the board the arms should be driven forward and upwards until they are in line with the head. It is often effective to ask the gymnast to pull one shoulder and the corresponding hip back to initiate the twist from the board. In reality this backward movement is accompanied by forward movement of the opposite hip and shoulder, but this is a useful way to convey an image of the type of movement and body shape required.

It is very important that when the gymnast makes contact with the horse, her shoulder angle is fully extended, and the body slightly arched. Both these factors will increase the effectiveness of the 'snap action'. This snap action from the top of the horse should follow the same technique as that used in the round-off and in the back handspring. All the muscles down the front of the body are on stretch, so when they are asked to contract they do so very quickly.

There is a compression phase followed by a repulsion phase

Gymnasts with predominantly fast twitch fibres will be able to generate forces more rapidly than their slow-twitch colleagues and thus need less time in contact with the horse. Ideally, gymnasts should leave the horse before reaching the vertical; if they leave after the vertical, they will not maximise the height or length of the vault.

Once the gymnast has left the top of the horse, there is no advantage in leaving the arms above the head; they can be brought down to the thighs or the knees, depending on whether the gymnast is doing a straight, tuck or pike position in second flight.

The gymnast should extend the body to a straight line before landing. When she does so will depend upon the amount of rotation and height created from the top of the horse. The more rotation and height, the earlier the gymnast can safely extend.

Mechanics of the vault

The force (Fr) acts behind the gymnast's CG at a perpendicular distance (d). This causes rotation. In the diagram, if the resultant force were to go through the gymnast's CG there would be no rotation when she left the board. The further the resultant force is from the CG, measured perpendicularly, the greater the rotation.

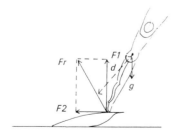

A torque twist is initiated on the board, causing the gymnast to complete a half twist before she reaches the horse. As she contacts the horse, she applies forces to it as a result of her motion (translational/rotational). She also applies forces to the horse as a result of muscular contraction (the 'snap action'). In both cases the forces contribute to the height and rotation of the second flight phase. Once airborne, the gymnast can increase her rate of rotation about her CG by changing from a straight body to a tucked or piked shape.

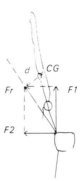

Resultant reaction forces

The rotation created can now be accelerated by the long lever of the body being made smaller by tucking or piking of the legs.

Progressions

Key points

- Speed of run-up.
- Completed half-on.
- Shoulder and hip angles must be *open* when contacting the horse.
- They *both* must 'snap' simultaneously to create rotation.
- The gymnast should ideally leave the horse before she reaches the vertical.

1.   Standing on the floor, the gymnast should swing her arms forwards and upwards above her head. It is often useful to ask the gymnast to 'pull one shoulder and hip back' to ensure that the twist is achieved with the arms parallel, and not crossed in front of the head. Remember that in fact as one shoulder moves back, the other moves forwards.

2.   Now she should take one step, swing the arms forwards and half turn onto her hands. The number of steps can then be increased to add greater dynamics to the practice.

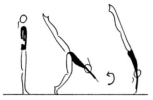

3. The same action can now be performed on to a box top from a springboard.

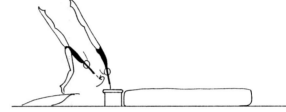

4. To feel some flight off the hands, as well as rotation, a trampette can replace the box and the gymnast can rotate onto her back.

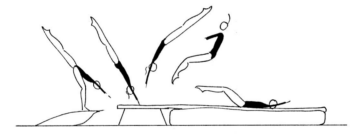

5. Using a spotting belt, the gymnast should go to handstand on the floor; as she snaps her body to create height and rotation she will be lifted through 540° of lateral axis rotation by the spotting belt to land on her feet. A coach will have to give the gymnast some additional lift from her hands to help create height and rotation.

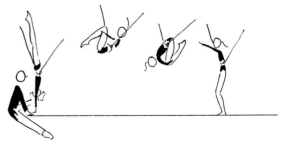

6. The gymnast should now experience the half-on and thrust-off, using a run and a two-footed take-off. This can be done using a trampette or a springboard and safety landing modules.

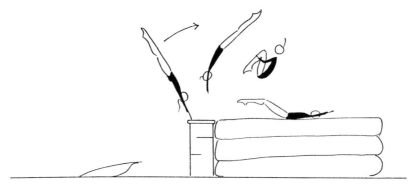

7. The gymnast should now attempt to re-create progression 6, but with the body dished in the second flight. When she has created enough height and rotation to land on her shoulders, she should be physically ready to attempt the vault in the tuck position.

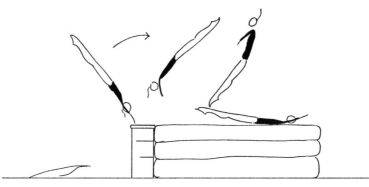

8. When the gymnast is attempting the vault, at least one coach, if not two, should stand in on the landing side of the horse. The coach should put his/her near hand (i.e. the hand closest to the horse) on the upper stomach of the gymnast whilst his/her far hand should go on the gymnast's lower back.

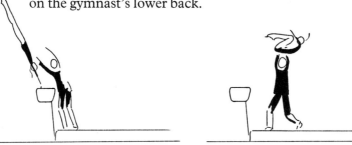

Specific conditioning

1. The following diagram shows a gymnast with her upper body in an arched position and her lower body horizontal and supported by the

wall bars. This upper body shape represents the shape she will be in when she is in contact with the horse. In the vault she has to contract the upper body very vigorously to create height and rotation. In the exercise she has to recreate the same shapes in the upper body, eventually with speed.

2. When the gymnast has made contact with the horse she should be in the shape shown below. It is important to condition the muscles using the exact shapes and rates of contractions that will be required of them in the vault. Have the gymnast move quickly from a to b, hold the position for a second and then lower slowly to c.

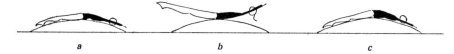

a   b   c

3. Get the gymnast to lie over the end of a horse with some weight on her legs. Ask her to lift up to just past the horizontal line and twist the upper body to the left and right on alternative repetitions.

Round-off vault (Yurchenko vault)

Until the round-off vault came along all vaults were dynamic: they required good speed down the runway and very fast reactions off the springboard. The Russian gymnast Natalia Yurchenko introduced the round-off vault, which became very popular in the mid-1980s. Gymnasts can achieve this vault without being very dynamic down the runway or on the board. The less powerful gymnast now has the ability to compete with high-quality vaults.

Before learning this vault, the gymnast must have a very sound round-off back handspring. Any existing problems will only be exaggerated; they will not disappear.

It still holds true that the faster, more powerful gymnast will perform this vault more dynamically, and therefore ideally the run-up for this vault should be as fast as possible, although under control. When the gymnast arrives on the board she should land just short of the vertical, with the

body in a straight line, and the knees slightly bent. There will be a depression phase on the board during which the gymnast continues to rotate until the springboard recoils and the legs extend, finally resulting in the gymnast leaving the board.

For the gymnast to land on the springboard at the required angle she must first perform a round-off. When the gymnast places her hands on the floor she has the option of making anything from a 90° turn to a 180° turn. Due to the anatomical range of movement of the wrist and the pressures being exerted, an angle of about 45° with the second hand turned in seems to be optimal.

The hands need to be placed sufficiently far from the leading foot to ensure that there is no shoulder angle during the round-off.

It must be remembered that the gymnast will be performing the round-off up an incline to a level of 20 cm higher than the ground. An extremely forceful thrust from the hands is required to enable the gymnast to land on the springboard just short of vertical. Clearly, taller gymnasts have an advantage at this stage. Good shoulder alignment (keeping the shoulder angle fully open) means that the gymnast can resist the pressure of the floor at high speed.

When the gymnast leaves the springboard to start her pre-flight phase she should think of lifting her hips and driving her hands towards the horse. The head should stay between the arms but should be allowed to rotate to look for the top of the horse. On contact with the horse there should be no shoulder angle and the body should be in a slight arch. There is a compression phase, during which time the gymnast is still in contact with the horse, rotating around her wrists. At this time the

Elena Shushunova, USSR

gymnast consciously changes body shape to a slightly 'dished' position. The more dynamic gymnast will do this well before the vertical line, but all gymnasts should leave the horse by the vertical. A balance must be struck between height and length of the vault. This can be achieved by changing the angle at which the gymnast comes onto the vault, which in turn affects the point at which she leaves the vault, and the shape of her flight path (parabolic curve).

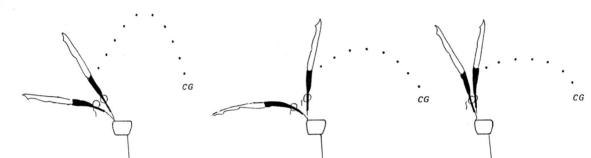

Post-flight will depend on the sequence of events which has preceded it. Most powerful gymnasts run so hard and create so much rotation from the springboard that they could do the whole vault and land on their feet without ever touching the horse. Considering the complexity of the vault and the number of variables present, this ability is desirable. Slower gymnasts need to thrust from the vaulting horse to create the necessary rotation. The 'dish' shape the gymnast creates as she leaves the horse should be maintained throughout the post-flight. The arms should drop to the thighs to help rotation by reducing the moment of inertia about the somersault axis. Even if the gymnast has insufficient rotation to stay straight and needs to pike or tuck, the initial position off the top of the vault should be the same.

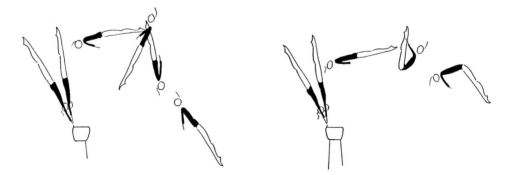

When the gymnast lands, the arms should move forwards and sideways to aid stability. The body should assume a plié position to absorb the landing forces gradually.

Mechanics of the move

The mechanics of the round-off and back handspring are the same as those of the round-off and back handspring on the floor. The magnitude of the vertical and horizontal components of force will alter, but the principles are the same.

    As the gymnast makes contact with the horse she applies forces to it as a result of her translational and rotational motion. She also applies forces to the horse as a result of muscular contraction (the snap action). In both cases the forces contribute to the height and rotation of the second flight phase.

Net reaction forces

    When the gymnast leaves the horse the rotation point will change to her centre of gravity. If the arms, when leaving the horse, pull down hard to the thighs there will be an equal and opposite reaction of the legs coming up towards the arms, thus aiding rotation. The gymnast can increase her rate of rotation about her CG by reducing her moment of inertia, i.e. changing from a straight body shape to a tuck or pike shape.

Progressions

Key points

- Shoulder angle should be open when the hands make contact with the floor.
- The body should be vertical on the springboard.
- Shoulder and hip angle should be open when making contact with the horse.
- The gymnast must leave the horse on or before she reaches the vertical.

  1. From stand, the gymnast jumps to shoulder stand.

2. Back handspring to strike position on the horse. The coach should help to stop the gymnast in the 'memory' position. This is a point in the move that is very important due to its shape and/or relative position to the apparatus.

3. Strong hip elevation to strike position. The coach should assist elevation and stop the gymnast in the 'memory' position.

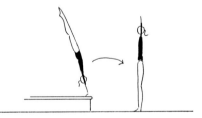

4. Kick to handstand and 'snap' to create height and elevation from the hands. The snap is a dynamic contraction of all the muscles down the front of the body.

5. The gymnast performs a back-flip on a platform to 'snap' through to lying. Start tucked, then piked and finally dished.

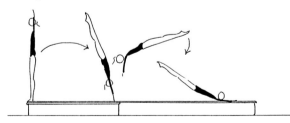

6. Round-off back handspring to land with the shoulders on a pile of safety landing modules. At this stage, check that the knees do not

travel in front of the feet (i.e. towards the toes) as the gymnast drives into the back handspring.

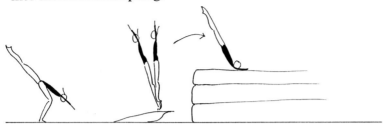

7. The same exercise as 6, but the gymnast should now land on her hands.

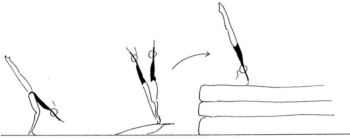

8. The gymnast should perform a round-off salto in the stretched position. This practice will check the knees again. In this practice a different shape and greater speed are introduced.

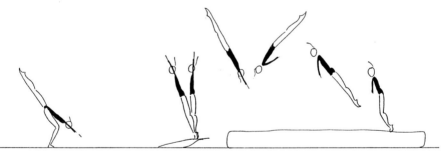

9. The safety landing modules can be re-introduced and the gymnast can now perform the round-off back handspring with hand contact to 'snap' through to her shoulders on the mats.

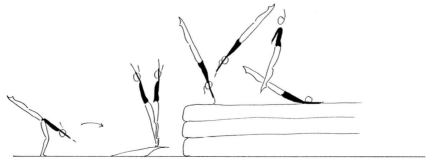

10. A horse can now be introduced. To keep the anxiety level as low as possible, wrap the horse in a thick mat.

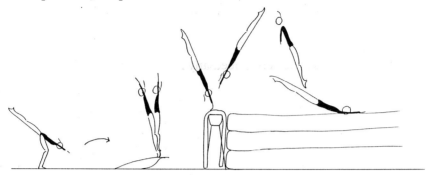

11. The same practice as 10, but with a thinner mat over the horse.
12. To encourage full commitment from the gymnast as she leaves the springboard, you can teach a stretched salto onto a pile of mats. A salto off, with or without twists, can help to orientate body positions for the desired post-flight.

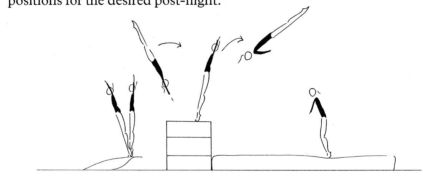

13. If a foam landing pit is available, the gymnast can perform a double salto, going through the body position changes necessary for the vault.

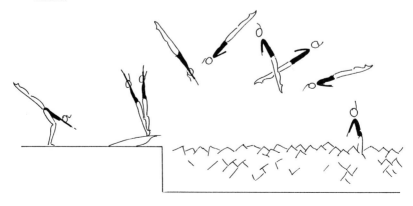

Specific conditioning

Before this vault can be performed successfully, gymnasts should first master the round-off, the back handspring and eventually the back salto. If the conditioning exercises have been correctly followed at each stage, the gymnasts should not need any further exercises.

13   The asymmetric bars

Float upstart (glide kip)

Probably the most important linkage on bars is the upstart. It takes many
forms: the short upstart, reverse upstart, long upstart, upstart to catch,
to mention but a few. The one most often taught first is the float upstart.
This move requires a very well-conditioned body. Too many gymnasts
try to learn it without being given enough 'fire power' to work with. Daily
practice of the move with a hand spotter is useful to get the rhythm.
This must be coupled with a good conditioning programme which helps
the gymnast to achieve the move in the least amount of time.

The gymnast should start by jumping towards horizontal and catching
the bar with the centre of gravity as high as possible.

Position (a) would be absolutely ideal but is alas unrealistic. If most
gymnasts could get to position (b) at the start of the upstart, this would
be pleasing. In this position gravity creates rotation for the gymnast and
she should pike as late as possible to miss the floor and continue the
float. The head should stay between the arms at all times, and the arms
must stay straight. There should be no shoulder angle until the end of
the float. If there is, the gymnast will lose her grip near the completion
of the upstart.

At the end of the float the feet stay parallel with the ground whilst
the hips and chest are lifted slightly. This stretch of all the muscles down
the front of the body will produce a fast reaction of a pike at the hips,
resulting in the ankles coming to the bar. The lifting of the hips and
chest also raises the gymnast's centre of gravity and therefore maximises
the energy available within the body to facilitate the upstart action. With
this super stretch position, the front of the ankles can come to the bar

Fan Di, China

rapidly. The faster this happens, the less time the hips will have to drop back under the bar. The less the hips drop back, the better the upstart.

From here the gymnast closes the shoulder angle as quickly as possible, driving the bar up the shin bones and thighs until she finishes the upstart. If the hips swing back vertically below and a distance from the bar, the chance of successfully achieving the move is negligible.

The finishing position of the upstart will depend on which element is to follow. If the gymnast wished to cast to handstand, she would stop the bar at the mid-thigh position, keeping her arms straight and allowing the shoulders to continue in front of the bar. She would then be ready to cast to handstand.

Mechanics of the upstart

As the gymnast jumps to catch the bar, her CG should be as high and as far from the bar as possible. This is achieved by jumping and catching the bar in a straight line as close to the horizontal as possible. Once this long lever has started to move it is then shortened by piking at the hips, allowing the feet to glide over the floor, but not to touch it. When a long lever in rotation shortens, it has the effect of accelerating the rotation.

CG

At the end of the forward swing, the legs are piked to the bar. At the same time the shoulder angle is closing to raise the body's CG.

The legs touch the bar, starting at the ankle and staying in contact with the bar until the upper thigh. The legs drive down hard and forcibly stop short of the vertical. This action creates a reaction in the upper body and it tries to move away from the bar. The bar, in turn, imparts a reaction force and pulls the shoulders over the bar.

Progressions

Key points

- The end of the float must be fully extended.
- Aim for a fast pike of the legs to the bar.
- Keep the leg in contact with the bar from the ankle to upper thigh.
- Press down on the bar with straight arms to get the shoulders over the bar.

1. Get the gymnast to jump and prepare for the float. The coach should stop her when she catches the bar. This should be a 'memory' position for the gymnast.

2. As for progression 1, then allow the gymnast to float foward to the stretch position.

3. Allow progression 2 to be continuous and support the end of the float. This is another 'memory' position.
4. Have the gymnast carefully positioned on a platform holding on to the bar. Her hips must be able to swing clear of the platform when she pikes. The coach helps her to lift her hips to extend the body before she pikes to the bar. The coach then supports her lower back and hamstrings to achieve the upstart.

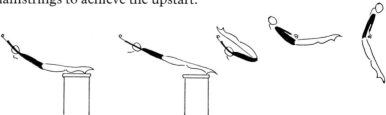

5. Ask the gymnast to swing backwards and forwards with her feet in a loop and then close the angle on the backswing to simulate the second half of the upstart, with concentration on the upper body.

6. The gymnast can perform the whole element. The coach's support will be needed for the end of the float so that the hips do not drop back too far while the ankles are moving to the bar. Then help the gymnast to keep her legs in contact with the bar, whilst taking some of the weight from the upper body to facilitate a good shoulder closure. Good rhythm is needed throughout this move.

Specific conditioning

1. Use elastics through the complete range of the shoulder joint.

2. Hanging from a bar, close the shoulder angle to invert the body. Some support will be needed for this exercise.

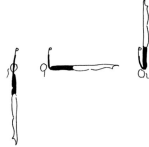

3. The hip flexor muscle group is not sufficiently efficient in raising the leg, and needs to be strengthened to cope with the necessary workload. Leg lifts to a bar will help.

4.   The 'V' sit exercise will help to produce speed of contraction.

Pirouette

In a good bar routine the gymnast must pass through the handstand. There are many techniques available for making a turn through the handstand, whether it be half or full turn. Two techniques in particular have become very popular. These are known as the 'top change' and the 'blind change' into the half turn.

Top change

This technique is generally accepted as the best to use when a gymnast casts to handstand from an upstart. Its advantage over most other techniques is that it can be initiated before the vertical and finish at the vertical. This allows the gymnast the choice of many exits. Most other techniques are completed after the vertical, with the result that the gymnast has to make some kind of a long swing action into the next move.

When the gymnast casts from the bar, her hands should be as close to hip width as possible. If the hands are wider apart, then the handstand is easier but the pirouette is significantly more difficult. When the gymnast has reached seven-eighths of her handstand, she must take the weight off (unweight) the hand she will be moving first. The same applies when a person standing astride wants to stand on one leg. If she does not unweight the leg, she falls over.

 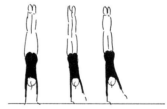

When the gymnast has cast to seven-eighths handstand she must extend through her right arm if she wishes to move the right hand first. This will shift the weight to the left hand, allowing the right hand to be taken off the bar and replaced in reverse grip, slightly closer to the left hand, to facilitate the turn. To keep a good line through the body, with tension, the right arm should be extended throughout the pirouette whilst the left arm reaches behind the head, making a half turn to the left. When the left hand returns to the bar the mass of the body centralises between the arms and the gymnast is ready to start the next element. In order to maintain good alignment of the body during the turn, it is important that the left arm does not go in front of the head. The turn should be completed by the time the gymnast has reached the vertical.

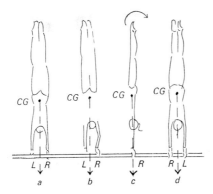

Mechanics of the move

In diagram (a) above, the CG is acting through the centre point of the base. Diagram (b) shows that a force has been applied to the bar through the right arm, making the CG move towards the left hand and allowing the right hand to leave the bar. As the CG did not come to rest directly above the support base, it will begin to move back to the right. Diagram (c) shows that the gymnast has replaced the right hand in reverse grip and is pirouetting on it. Before the left hand leaves the bar it can also apply a small force to the bar to aid the turn. Diagram (d) shows the gymnast having completed the turn; the CG has centralised itself once more between the hands.

Progressions

Key points

- Good body tension must be maintained throughout the move.
- Turn first hand and extend shoulder.
- Second hand reaches behind the head to avoid arms crossing in front of the face.

1. Ask the gymnast to face a flat wall with the front of the body touching the wall. Rotate the right hand outwards so that the back of the hand is on the wall. Push on the left hand and make the body rotate, with

Fan Di, China

the left shoulder going backwards. Make sure the body stays in contact with the wall.

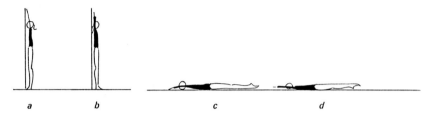

2. The same exercise, but using a horizontal surface.
3. The same exercise, but this time inclining the body by small degrees increasing each time until handstand is achieved. To avoid compression of the wrist joint, it is advisable to use a box top to lessen the angle at the wrist.

4. Get the gymnast to kick to handstand and keep transferring the weight from one hand to the other, lifting each hand off the floor for one second at a time.

5. Now ask the gymnast to reverse one of her hands after lifting it from the floor. Replace it with the fingers pointing in the opposite direction.

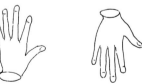

6. Repeat progression 5 and then ask the gymnast to complete the 180° turn.

7.   As soon as the move has been perfected on the floor, it can be taken to a bar just off the floor and then to a regulation height bar.

     In the early stages the coach should be prepared to handspot, both to shape the gymnast and to help with balance.

Specific conditioning

1.   Holding a handstand, assisted by the coach, and extending through one shoulder joint and then the other.

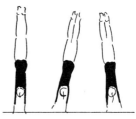

2.   Holding a handstand, assisted by the coach, closing and opening the shoulder angle.

Blind change

Most gymnasts opt for this technique when they wish to add a half or full turn on to the end of a circle move on the bar, such as a clear hip, giant, stalder, toe on and off to handstand. It can also be performed from a simple cast from the bar.

     When the gymnast has nearly completed the circle, she twists the body in the direction of the turn by pulling on the bar in the opposite direction. A common fault is for the gymnast to lose tension and twist turning the hips, but 'leaving the feet behind'. The coach should ask the gymnast

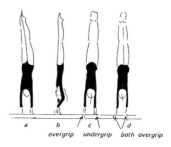

a   b   c   d
overgrip   undergrip   both overgrip

to move her feet in the direction of the turn to achieve the desired effect. At the same time, she must unweight the hand that is going to make the turn by extending through the shoulder of that arm.

As the gymnast is coming out of the circle and is moving towards handstand, she must consciously move the feet in the direction of the turn (a). It must be remembered that this element will move across the bar one body width; the move does not happen on the spot. In this example, the left arm is the support arm. It must stay straight and the gymnast will press down on it to aid the turn and help keep the line of the body (b). The body moves anti-clockwise towards the left arm. The right hand will grip the bar in overgrip, which means the gymnast will now be in mixed grip, because the left hand has yet to move (c). The left hand now changes on the spot to finish up in overgrip (d).

If the gymnast wished to complete a full pirouette, instead of placing the right hand on the bar in overgrip, she would place it in reverse grip and then complete the next half turn by moving just the left hand, as for a normal top change.

It is important to remember that if the gymnast wished to make a full pirouette, the blind change would need to go in the same direction as the top change which follows: if the right hand changed first in the top change, the right hand must change first in the blind change too.

Mechanics of the move

As the gymnast moves into the fourth quadrant of her circle there will be a point when the hands have become unweighted due to the extension towards handstand. At this point the gymnast tries to turn the bar clockwise, in the opposite direction to the intended turn. The reaction to this is that the body and legs turn clockwise. To complete the blind change, the gymnast should pull on the bar with her right hand, push on the bar with her left hand, resulting in an opposite and equal reaction from the bar and the gymnast pirouetting around her left hand.

This action would secure a half pirouette; the other half would follow the mechanics of the top change.

Progressions

Key points

- Move the feet in the direction of the turn.
- Keep the supporting arm and shoulder fully extended.
- Turn late.
- There should be no angle in the body after the turn.

1.   Backward roll to handstand on straight arms and straight legs.

2. Have the gymnast at 45° on her back and make her roll through 180° using the correct hand change. A box top or bar would decrease the compression on the wrist and therefore help to prevent injury.

3. From handstand, resting against the mats, get the gymnast to roll through 180° with the correct hand change. Then let her pike extension and turn through 180°. Try to encourage the gymnast to turn when she is not in contact with the mat.

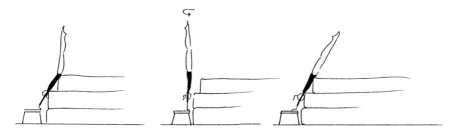

4. Backward roll to handstand with 180° turn. This will need to be done slowly at first, with support from a coach.

5. The extension and turn phase can be practised from a sprung surface, for example a mini-tramp (trampette) for small gymnasts, or double mini-tramp or trampoline, in all cases with a bar attachment.

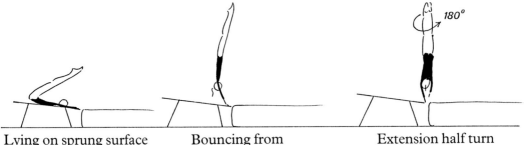

Lying on sprung surface   Bouncing from   Extension half turn
surface pike/extension

6.   The complete move with support from the coach. The coach should stand on a platform, hip high to the bar. He or she should be on the opposite side to the hand being released first, and should support the gymnast around the waist. The coach's far hand should move towards his/her body as the gymnast makes the turn.

Start of turn   Finish of turn

7.   Any gymnast wishing to learn the blind change from a giant circle needs to have a strong fast giant circle.
      She should make three preparatory swings on the bar, then half turn so that she is one body width further across the bar. This is initially done beneath the horizontal, then as more confidence is gained, at the horizontal and finally above the horizontal until the turn is made just short of handstand. When enough of these have been done for the gymnast to perform the move consistently she can then take the move over the bar, remembering that she will need to re-grasp the bar in reverse grip and not regular grip.

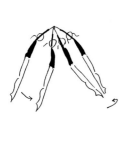
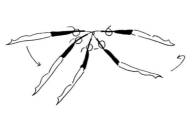
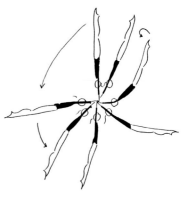

Specific conditioning

1. Ask the gymnast to lie on her back on the floor and raise her legs to an angle of 45°. Initially the arms should be placed sideways on the floor at shoulder height. Later on, they can be taken above the gymnast's head. Without lifting either shoulder from the floor she must twist her feet and hold them 10 cm from the ground on alternate sides.

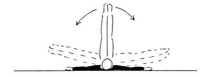

Back straddle

This move is probably one of the first release and re-catch moves the gymnast will learn. Taken to its full potential it becomes a move of great sophistication, but in its basic form it is comparatively simple.

The bars need to be relatively wide to make this move as simple as possible.

The gymnast should forward swing on the high bar to a horizontal position. The body should be straight, with a slight angle in the shoulders to enable the gymnast to maintain a good grip on the bar.

At the beginning of the backswing the body stays straight. Small gymnasts can lead with their hips until the bottom of the swing when they drive their heels into an arch shape which is followed by a piking and lifting of the hips. Taller gymnasts have difficulty when they lead with their hips, and so they normally lead with their heels.

The point of release depends upon how efficient the backswing was. The best release point is when the hips are nearing the level of the high bar.

At the point of release the gymnast can pull backwards on the bar, opening her shoulder angle slightly if she needs more rotation. On release the gymnast pikes as hard as she can to aid rotation and finish in support on the lower bar. At the same time, she should straddle her legs.

Mechanics of the move

At the end of the forward swing the gymnast's CG is as far as possible from the point of rotation (the bar), and at a distance (d1) from it.

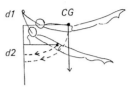

At the start of the backswing, the gymnast should attempt to keep her CG as far as possible from the centre of rotation (d1), thereby maximising the turning effect of gravity. By piking, the gymnast shortens her body (d2), reducing her moment of inertia about the bar and increasing her angular velocity.

At the bottom of the swing the gymnast drives her heels backwards to create an arch (b), pre-stretching the muscles down the front of the body to facilitate a fast pike (c). If the gymnast releases as her CG approaches the level of the high bar (d), she will have a relatively high flight path that provides enough time for her to rotate her torso and arms 90° downwards, with just enough length to travel backwards and catch the low bar.

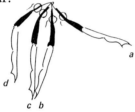

The diagram below shows the correct release (a) and an early release (b), in which the gymnast's CG has passed the bar before she catches it.

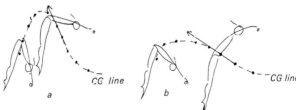

On release the gymnast stops rotating about the bar and starts rotating about her CG. Since she has a smaller moment of inertia about her CG (short lever), she will rotate more quickly in flight.

The gymnast has two ways of controlling rotation. She can open her shoulder angle further, exerting an upward force on the high bar. The high bar in turn exerts a downward reaction force on the gymnast, aiding her rotation. Or she can pike more deeply, shortening the lever even more and increasing the rate of rotation.

For safety reasons it is important that the gymnast does not close her shoulder angle and push down on the high bar. This causes rotation in a backward direction which could result in the gymnast not catching the low bar.

Progressions

Key points

- A forward swing to the horizontal.
- An arch pike in the backswing.
- Hips should be the highest part of the body after release from the high bar.

1. This move is all about swinging, so a single bar with the gymnast making the basic swing shapes would be a good place to start.

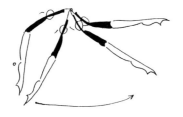 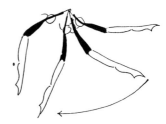

2. When the shape is correct the low bar should be introduced so that the gymnast can backswing to stand on the bar. Initially a mat may be needed to cover the low bar.

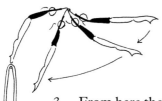

3. From here the gymnast can release the high bar, pike to the low bar, take weight through the arms and lift the legs clear of the bar.

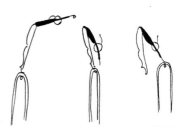

4. Now stack some safety landing modules up to the height of the low bar and the gymnast can attempt the complete move.

5. As soon as the gymnast is confident and is bearing weight on the arms, the mats can be removed one at a time until she completes the move. The mat over the low bar can be removed at any time when you and the gymnast are happy with the development of the work.

Specific conditioning

Swinging moves should not require a great deal of specific conditioning. If the gymnast were to catch the low bar and then wished to straddle float, stomach and hip flexor strengthening would be applicable. It might also be helpful for the gymnast to develop enough strength to control the straddle shape. For any gymnast wishing to finish in handstand, shoulder strengthening and tension exercises would be required.

1. The gymnast lies on the floor on her back, then supports herself on her elbows. This position takes the strain off the lower back when the legs are raised 10 cm. Now get her to do scissor actions, alternately crossing the legs on each scissor.

2. Using the asymmetric bars, have the gymnast hang from the high bar facing the low bar. When the gymnast is new to the exercise, padding the low bar is advisable.

   The gymnast should close the shoulder angle to 90° whilst straddling the legs over the low bar and bringing them together. As soon as they are together, the legs must straddle again so that the gymnast does not hit the bar.

Short clear hip circle (free hip, clear hip)

The best position from which to start this move is the handstand (a).
The gymnast should take advantage of gravity to rotate the body about
the shoulders through 90° from handstand to the horizontal (b). The
gymnast should not move the shoulders forward to counterbalance this
action.

If the gymnast kicks into the circle before the horizontal, the timing
generally leaves her short of the handstand. If she kicks into the circle
past the horizontal, the timing generally puts her past the handstand. At
horizontal the legs are kicked at the bar, forming a slight pike, whilst
the shoulders are closed as hard and as fast as possible to direct the upper
body backwards and downwards (c – d).

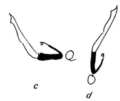

The bar should not touch the leg (it would not be a clear circle), but
a point mid-thigh comes close as the legs move towards the bar. This
open pike position is held until the feet just pass the vertical line passing
through the bar (e). At this point, the bar, which has bent during the
circle, bends a little more as the hips extend to the straight line. On the
recoil of the bar the gymnast is lifted towards handstand. As the hip angle
extends, the gymnast very quickly extends through the shoulder joint as
well. These actions subsequently unweight the hands and enable the
gymnast to take a new grip on top of the bar (f – j).

Mechanics of the move

From handstand, the gymnast's first axis of rotation is a line passing
through the shoulders. The body should be kept as straight as possible
so that the gymnast's CG is as far from the point of rotation as it can
be. This ensures that the turning effect of gravity is as great as possible
and consequently the angular velocity created will also be as great as
possible (1).

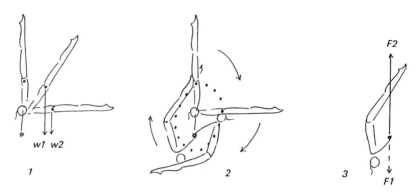

When the body is at the horizontal, the gymnast begins to rotate about the bar in addition to rotating about her shoulders. At this point the closure of the shoulder angle and slight pike brings the gymnast's CG closer to the bar. This action will accelerate the gymnast's progress around the bar since a 'long lever' has been shortened.

The body should now have sufficient rotation to go around the bar and back to handstand. To do this the CG must be lifted to its highest position (2). The hip and shoulder angles extend, exerting a force (F1) on the bar. The bar exerts a reaction force of the same magnitude on the gymnast (F2). This reaction force sends the CG out of its orbit around the bar and up towards handstand (3).

Progressions

Key points

- The gymnast must maintain good body tension.
- Very fast shoulders are essential from the horizontal through to handstand.
- Arms must be held straight throughout the move.

1. From handstand on a floor bar, the gymnast falls through 90° to a safety landing module. Shoulders stay vertically above the bar, and must not move in front of it.

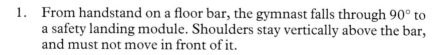

2. This is the same practice as 1, but done initially on a floor bar, and then done on a low bar with the coach stopping the legs.

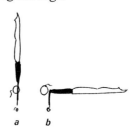

3.　The gymnast does an undershoot with one leg leading (a) and the second leg joining the first (b). Concentration should be on body alignment and tension. The shoulder angle opens, (d) but the rest of the body must stay fixed.

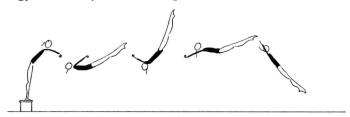

　　　a　　　*b*　　*c*　　　*d*　　　　*e*　　　　　*f*

4.　This is the same action as 3, but from both feet together. The gymnast may start from a platform in order to achieve some height.

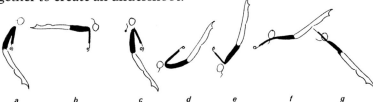

5.　From front support (a), the gymnast should cast to the horizontal and be stopped by the coach in this position (b). It is a 'memory' position for the gymnast. There are two other 'memory' positions which the gymnast should be stopped in. These are at (c) and (d). When these static positions have been learned the gymnast can join them together to create an undershoot.

　　a　　　　　*b*　　　　　*c*　　　*d*　　　*e*　　　　*f*　　　*g*

6.　The same practice as 5, but the gymnast casts to handstand, or is put in the position and falls to the horizontal where the coach just 'checks' the speed, i.e. slows it down slightly and then allows the gymnast to do the undershoot.

7.　Get the gymnast to backward hip circle so that she can concentrate on trying to increase her speed of wrist change, i.e. a rapid change from being dragged around the bar to being on top of the bar.

8.　The gymnast must now learn to push on her hands to raise the body to clear support. A coach is needed to stop the legs and support the chest or shoulder initially.

    If the gymnast fails to wrist change fast enough she will not be able to achieve this progression.

9.   The backward roll to handstand on straight arms is useful for the shoulder extension work.

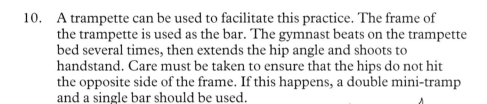

10. A trampette can be used to facilitate this practice. The frame of the trampette is used as the bar. The gymnast beats on the trampette bed several times, then extends the hip angle and shoots to handstand. Care must be taken to ensure that the hips do not hit the opposite side of the frame. If this happens, a double mini-tramp and a single bar should be used.

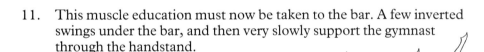

11. This muscle education must now be taken to the bar. A few inverted swings under the bar, and then very slowly support the gymnast through the handstand.

12. Ask the gymnast to perform the clear circle towards handstand from a platform or horizontal cast. Emphasise straight arm action throughout. Support the abdominal and lumbar areas.

13. Finally, using the same support technique, the gymnast can attempt the element from handstand.

Specific conditioning

There are three major muscle actions in this move: to keep the shoulder angle closed at the bottom of the downswing; to open the shoulder angle on the upswing; and to keep extremely good body tension throughout.

1. The gymnast should perform a backward roll to handstand on straight arms, and lower to front support.

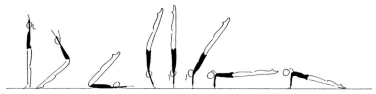

2. Using the trolley trainer (a platform on wheels that runs up and down tracks on an inclined runway), ask the gymnast to open the shoulder angle with speed.

3. Tension exercises should be done slowly, with good control. Straight body, then lift and lower, leading with the hips on the lift and with the heels on the lower stage.

4. Shoulders and feet on a raised surface, moving the body from a slight arch to a slight sag position. This must be done facing upwards and downwards.

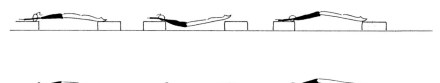

Giant circle

Over the last few years, the physical dimensions of the asymmetric bars have become wider and wider. The giant circle has therefore become less

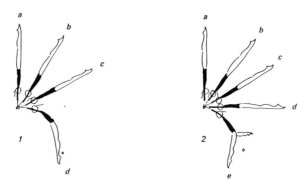

difficult and has become a core move in women's Artistic Gymnastics, as it has always been in men's Artistic Gymnastics. Every bar routine in every major competition has at least one giant circle in it. The move should start in handstand and then fall off-balance for as long as possible before the body has to change shape to pass the low bar (1a–c). The move can be done with the legs together throughout the move, or passing through a straddle position as the body passes the low bar (2a–d).

If the gymnast can pass through complete box splits (i.e. 180° through a forward split position), then she can fall further in the downswing to the point (2d); otherwise the change of body shape has to happen at the point 1c.

After the body passes the low bar, in its concave upper body shape, both techniques are the same. The gymnast should try to drive the heels backwards underneath the low bar whilst thrusting the hips forwards underneath the high bar. There should be no shoulder angle at this point. The bottom of the swing is the fastest point of the circle and some gymnasts are not strong enough to hold the shoulder angle, resulting in it opening quickly and the gymnast 'ripping off' the bar.

It is virtually impossible to get the heels behind the bar, but the gymnast should attempt to do so. If she has performed this phase correctly the feet should kick hard and be directed over the high bar. Hip and shoulder angles will both occur at this point (3b). The speed of rotation around the bar will dictate the amount of angle necessary in the body to produce the move. This rotation speed will also dictate when the hip and shoulder angle can be fully extended to finish the element in handstand (3c–d).

Mechanics of the move

The gymnast should start in handstand so that her CG is as high and as far from the bar as is possible. This will ensure the greatest amount of angular momentum on the downswing.

She should fall for as long as possible in the extended shape before she has to change her body shape to miss the low bar. This again ensures the greatest amount of angular momentum. Whether she straddles or pikes past the low bar, she should do so as close to the low bar as possible. This maximises the angular momentum she is able to develop during the downswing and leaves good time to extend the hips forward.

This pre-stretching of the hip flexors facilitates the kick and adds to the angular momentum of the upswing. It also helps to reduce the distance of the CG from the bar. This is necessary to reduce the retarding effect of gravitational torque on the upswing.

In the diagram below, gymnast A shows a straight body throughout the move but will not make it back to handstand due to friction and air resistance. Gymnast B stays straight on the downswing, maximising her angular momentum. A very slight extension and kick through the bottom of the swing will ensure that she makes the final handstand, due to the accelerated swing and the CG coming closer to the bar and reducing the effect of gravitational torque. Gymnast C cannot stay straight during the complete downswing because of the position of the low bar. Maximum angular momentum cannot be achieved and therefore a greater shoulder and hip angle will have to be made to bring her CG even closer to the bar than that of B.

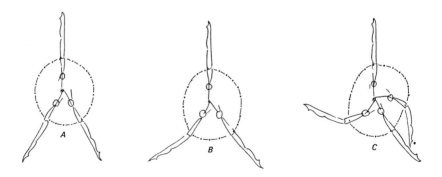

Natalia Yurchenko, USSR

Progressions

Key points

- Long stretched fall from handstand.
- Strong arch/tap between the bars.
- Shoulder and hip closure on the upswing.
- Arms should be straight throughout.

1. Using a floor bar, the gymnast should go to handstand, then fall with good form to the angle necessary for her to pike or straddle past the low bar.

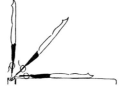

To finish in straddle   To finish straight, ready to pike

2. Basic body shaping in swings on the single bar.

3. When the gymnast has mastered progression 2 above, ask her to do three swings, and on the third to backward hip circle the bar to finish in front support. Some emphasis should be put on a fast wrist change from beneath the bar to above the bar when the hip circle is being performed.

4. Ask the gymnast to stand on the low bar, jump and swing between the bars and finish in the same position as progression 3.

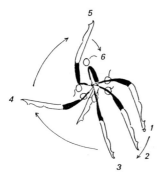

5. To emphasise the wrist change, ask the gymnast to perform many backward hip circles around the bar. Then support the legs at the end of the circle to get the gymnast into a support position with her body at the horizontal.

6. Now ask the gymnast to repeat progression 3, but with more swing. Before her legs touch the bar the coach should support them and take the gymnast across the bar similar to progression 5.

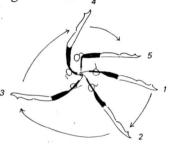

7. Get the gymnast to backward roll to handstand on straight arms.

8. Place a single bar across a tightly sprung trampoline and secure it to the frame. Holding on to the bar, the gymnast can practise the shape changes necessary in the fourth quadrant of the circle.

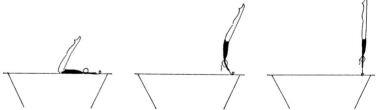

9. The gymnast should practise the downswing from handstand to a pile of soft mats. It is important to get the legs as close to the low bar as possible. The edge of the mat should be the imaginary bar.

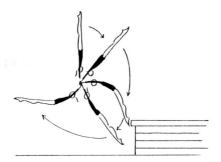

10. From handstand on the high bar, the gymnast should do a three-quarter circle to front support. Great care must be taken to secure the hands to the bar. It may be useful to use 'loops' or wrist straps at this point.

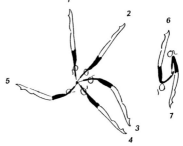

11. Now that the whole move has been experienced in part, it is time to put it together on a single bar. Support is still needed for the work in the fourth quadrant.

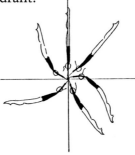

12. Once the move has been successfully completed as in (11), the stack of mats can be re-introduced to simulate the low bar. Emphasis should be put on the late and close movement of the feet to the mats and the direction of the kick over the high bar.

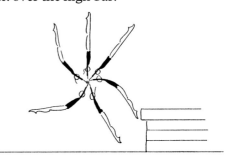

When all these progressions have been successfully completed, the gymnast can use asymmetric bars, with a protective padding over the low bar in the initial stages.

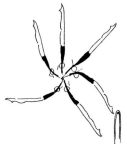

Specific conditioning

1. Tension exercises are necessary to keep the body in specific shapes whilst rotating around the bar. Lowering and lifting of the body whilst the gymnast holds a floor bar is useful for the work in the first quadrant of the circle. The coach should start with one arm across the shins of the gymnast and the other across her waist. As the gymnast gets stronger the coach can move the support further towards the feet.

2. Using the asymmetric bars, get the gymnast to move from a long hang position to a horizontal one, with the legs passing through the straddle position to miss the low bar. This exercise is useful for the third quadrant of the circle.

3. Using a floor bar or the end of a springboard, the gymnast should hold a handstand. With support, get her to take her shoulders forward, creating a shoulder angle, and then return to the straight handstand. This exercise will help in the fourth quadrant of the circle.

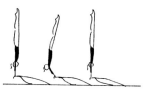

Stretched backward salto dismount (backaway)

In modern gymnastics, about three-quarters of all dismounts come from the backaway family.

The downswing from handstand to the point of release is exactly the same as that taught in the giant circle. To recap briefly, this means to fall for as long as possible (a–b), kick hard to miss the low bar (c), extend the hips forward (d) and then kick into the third quadrant, closing the hip and shoulder angles.

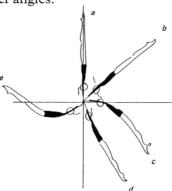

At the point of release the shoulder angle should be fixed. However, in some cases the gymnast may need to control her rotation by changing her shoulder angle just before release. Pulling back on the bar and opening her shoulder angle will reduce the rotation in the somersault, whilst closing the shoulder angle will increase it. The gymnast's aim should be to complete the somersault with as much height as possible. By varying her shoulder angle she can produce a rate of rotation appropriate to such a somersault.

From their initial position above the head, the arms should move slightly forwards and sideways in preparation for landing.

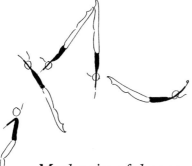

Mechanics of the move

The mechanics of the downswing of this move are exactly the same as for the giant circle.

The point of release and the actions the gymnast performs just prior to release are important since they determine the direction of the gymnast's CG and hence its flight path. At release, the gymnast's CG travels at a tangent to the curved path it followed whilst she was in contact with the bar. In a gravity-free environment, the CG would continue along this straight line. However, the effect of gravity results in the gymnast's

CG following a parabolic pathway that cannot be altered unless an external force acts on it.

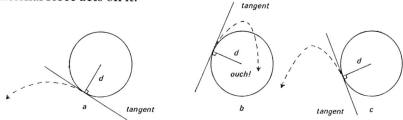

If the release point is early, the gymnast's CG will follow a low and long pathway (a). If release is late, then the flight path of the CG will be much higher, but shorter and towards the bar (b). If the gymnast releases the bar when her CG is at (c), just short of the horizontal, she will achieve good height and she will also have sufficient length to miss the bar.

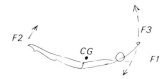

Just before release, the gymnast has the option of increasing or decreasing rotation by applying forces to the bar.

If the gymnast opens her shoulder angle, pulling back on the bar with a force (F1), the bar will exert a force of equal magnitude in the opposite direction on the gymnast (F3). This force acts against the angular motion the gymnast already possesses, thus reducing her rotation.

If the gymnast closes her shoulder angle by pressing on the bar, the force (F1) would enhance the angular motion of the gymnast and increase the rotation of the body.

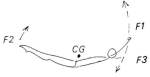

Progressions

Key points

- A strong downswing.
- Hip and shoulder closure prior to release.
- Good body tension after release.

1. Hold the gymnast just prior to the point of release, making sure her body shape is correct. Take her off the bar and rotate her slowly to complete the salto.

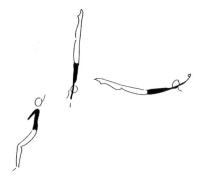

2. Now get the gymnast to do the same practice as (1), but using three preparatory swings. Initially you should stop her just prior to the release point before continuing the salto.
3. When the gymnast can dismount by herself from three swings, the low bar can be introduced. Ask her to stand on the low bar, jump from it and dismount making the correct shapes when passing the low bar. The release point, and the shape of the body at this point, still need to be emphasised.

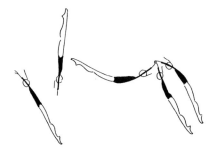

4. The gymnast should now start casting from the high bar until she can finally perform the element from handstand.

Specific conditioning

As mentioned already, this element is very similar to the giant circle. All the conditioning exercises used for the giant circle are useful for preparing the gymnast for the swing down from handstand to the point just before release.

A practice to develop spatial and kinaesthetic awareness for this backward salto which is moving forwards would be very useful, but it is very difficult to simulate this 'action'. Some forward landing practices from a height may be useful. These could be incorporated with landing conditioning practices from a height.

Elke Heine, FRG

14 The balance beam

In the competitive world of women's gymnastics it is generally the exercise on the balance beam that is the deciding factor in winning or losing a competition.

Three kinds of receptors are involved in learning a skill: exterioceptors, interioceptors and proprioceptors. Stimuli for the exterioceptors include the eye (there are over 120 million sensory elements in the retina alone) and those parts of the ear concerned with hearing. The interioceptors include the alimentary tract and the lungs, whilst the proprioceptors are found in the muscles, ligaments and joints.

Vision helps to give information about the body's position in relation to space. This means that if a gymnast performs a move on the beam and can see the landing, this information can be used to correct any faults which occur due to her position in space. If, for example, a gymnast were to perform a salto on the beam, she would see the take-off and its direction. She would also hear the take-off; and the muscles, tendons and ligaments would feel the take-off. The ear, too, can give a sensation of rotation. This feedback to the brain allows it to make decisions. These decisions should allow the gymnast to anticipate a certain kind of landing, and maybe certain types of correction. The more time there is to make these decisions, the more success can be experienced. The quicker she can see the beam again before landing, to add more information to that already gained on take-off, the better will be her chance of staying on.

There is little evidence to suggest that static balance and dynamic balance have any correlation and so both will need to be practised separately. The more time spent practising balance through its components, the sooner the movement can be downgraded from the conscious to the automatic. This should allow a better performance to occur.

The mental state of an athlete can greatly affect the execution of a movement demanding high levels of co-ordination. Errors can and do occur under physical or mental stress.

Fundamental locomotor movements

All these movements are initially taught on the floor and then taken to the beam at various heights. They include walking, running, hopping, skipping, sliding and galloping steps.

The gymnast should be taught to extend the feet from the beam, keeping them turned out, and place them back on the beam, turned out. The hips should be kept square to the direction of movement and the shoulders relaxed and again square to the direction of movement. The head should be kept erect and in line with a straight back. The gymnast should be allowed to drop the eye-line to catch the information needed for balance and beam length, so long as this does not affect the posture of the head.

When the gymnast is performing the moves backwards, there is a higher level of proprioceptive feedback and a diminished level of eye feedback. With the feet well turned out the gymnast will feel the edges of the beam and react to them quickly. The length of the beam behind the gymnast will be calculated by eye contact with the length of the beam in front, and by feeling for the end of the beam with the foot.

Jumps

All jumps and leaps begin and end with a good demi-plié. There are two reasons for this. First, it prepares the legs for a good thrust phase; and second, it absorbs the shock on landing.

The shoulders should be relaxed throughout the movement, with the head held erect. Many different arm positions can be used, but initially leaving them down by the side reduces variables.

Turns

Turns can be performed on one or both feet. A two-footed turn is, of course, more stable because of the extended base. Turns can be initiated from a step directly onto the ball of the foot (relévé) or from a demi-plié onto the ball of the foot. Various trunk, arm and head positions can be used, but initially a straight trunk with the head erect and the arms by the side is desirable. It is important to remember that the gymnast's weight (centre of gravity) must be directly above the point of rotation, i.e. the ball of the foot, throughout the movement. The classical way of teaching the head turn is for it to move last and arrive first. As gymnasts generally only do a half or full turn, some coaches have taught this element by keeping the head moving with the shoulders, with some success.

Acrobatics on the beam

Gymnasts need to be confident about their ability to perform elements on the beam. When a gymnast is first learning a move it should be done

Yang Bo, China

on the floor. The coach is in an ideal position to spot, with both feet firmly placed on the floor. A great deal of hand spotting and shaping should be done at this stage. The gymnast's confidence will grow quickly and her anxieties will be minimised. As soon as the move has been learned perfectly it can be transferred to a line on the floor. Physical support should now not be necessary and analytical coaching can be done from a distance. When the gymnast has mastered the move in this situation she can go on to a low beam. Once the move can be done perfectly on the low beam, the beam can be raised gradually until it is at competition height.

Your major consideration should be to ensure that the gymnast remains confident at each stage. If at any stage the gymnast cannot make herself attempt the move, then this is a clear signal that the situation is psychologically too demanding. Whilst the coach may be the best judge of technical correctness, the gymnast is the best judge of how she feels about performing a skill in a particular environment. For this reason you should let the gymnast say how much matting she wants under or over the beam. Sometimes you will need to devise a totally new practice to bridge the gap between a progression the gymnast has mastered, and the next logical practice. It is useful, at the end of the session, to talk and mutually agree the next goal for the next time the move is being worked. The gymnast can then prepare herself mentally for the next session.

Acrobatic moves on the beam are all about power and flexibility. How these moves are taught depends on how powerful and flexible the gymnast is. For example, if an inflexible gymnast wishes to perform a standing stretched salto backwards, she would need a great deal of power to create sufficient height and time to complete the move. More flexible, less powerful gymnasts would have to create more rotation than height. The ideal gymnast who has both can go for the optimum height and rotation. Whether the move stays on the beam or not is all about alignment.

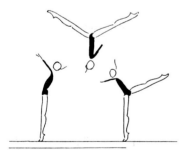 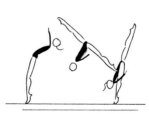 

Power without flexibility (height)   Flexibility without power (rotation)   Flexibility with power (height and rotation)

If the gymnast were under-powered and inflexible, then an accelerator such as a round-off or a flip would have to be used.

15　The floor

Handstand

This is the most important move in gymnastics. It is performed on all four pieces of apparatus, with and without pirouette.

The gymnast should start in a standing position with her body as long as possible, checking the knees are pressed back, the lower back is straight, the chest is in, the shoulders are down, and the arms are extended shoulder width apart above the head, with the head in a neutral position looking forward (a).

Ask the gymnast to lean forward until the pressure on the toes cannot stop her from falling over (b). At this point move one leg forward into a lunge (c). The chest should almost be on the leading thigh (d).

a b　　　c　　　　　　d　　e　　f

The gymnast should be in a straight line from the fingertips through the trunk of the body and down the leading leg. Just before the gymnast puts her hands on the floor she must extend through her shoulders. When the gymnast is in handstand she should still be in a straight line (f). Generally the head should be held so that the thumbs can just be seen. Any major movements of the head should be avoided as they may result in a pike or hollow of the body. However, slight movements of the head can be used to trim the line of the body.

The fingers should be well spread when the gymnast is holding the handstand, for it is their pressure on the floor which controls the balance.

Mechanics of the move

When the gymnast makes contact with the floor, the hands are the point of rotation.

The support leg pushes backwards, causing a ground reaction force

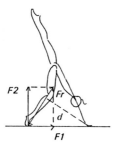

that has components acting forwards (F1) and upwards (F2). The resultant reaction force acts at a perpendicular distance (d) from the point of support i.e. the hands, and produces rotation about the hands.

The body can be looked upon as many segments stacked one upon the other. As long as the CG of the segments is located vertically above the support, a balance will be held.

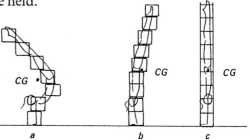

It is aesthetically more pleasing to see shape (c) than either (a) or (b). A slight deviation in (c) may be corrected easily: the deviation in (a) or (b) may not. Position (c) is the easiest to maintain because the CG of each box lies vertically above the next. Any minor correction needed to stop the handstand overbalancing forwards can be made by the wrist flexors exerting a pressure through the fingers on to the floor. The reaction from the floor is eccentric to the rotation point and so slight rotation occurs to save the situation. To avoid overbalancing in the opposite direction, the wrist extensor muscles contract to put pressure on the heel of the hands.

Progressions

Key points

- Good body alignment.
- Tension down the front and back of the body.
- Balance corrections are made by pressure on the fingertips.

1. A headstand. It is important for the gymnast to develop her kinaesthetic and spatial awareness, so that she knows where each part

Svetlana Boginskaya, USSR

of her body is in relation to its other parts, and in relation to the area around her.

2. From a squat position, with the shoulder angle extended, jump to a tucked handstand. This action emphasises the same aspects as progression 1.

3. A handstand with support. A great deal of shaping of the body is done at this stage.

4. A handstand against a wall, facing in.

5. A handstand with the feet in a small circular hoop. This practice develops spatial awareness as well as body form. The idea is not to touch the ring. Corrections should be made by using pressure on the fingertips.

Specific conditioning

1. Position the gymnast's shoulders and feet on platforms 30 cm off the mats. The gymnast's trunk should move slowly from a slight arch

Perfect one-arm balance: Olga Strajeva, USSR

to a slight curve. This exercise should be done with the face down
(a) and then up (b).

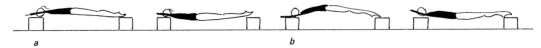

a   *b*

    If the exercise is too difficult for the gymnast when the platforms
are at the extremities of the body, move them closer together until
the exercise can be done correctly.

2.   From a shoulder stand, slowly lower the body to the floor, ensuring
that the feet touch the ground first.

Forward walkover

This move can only be demonstrated well by very flexible gymnasts. Like
the backward walkover, this move is performed on the beam as well as
on the floor and requires a great deal of balance in its latter stages. The
entry into the walkover can be done in many ways, some more
aesthetically pleasing than others. For simplicity, and to use the least
number of variables, the gymnast should start with both feet together
and the arms above the head. The shoulders should be relaxed at this
point, not level with the ears. The gymnast should lean forwards until
she goes off balance. At this point she should take a long lunge step,
extend through the shoulders and place the hands on the floor.

    When the hands are on the floor the support leg continues to extend
until it is straight, whilst the first leg keeps moving forward until a splits
position is achieved (a).

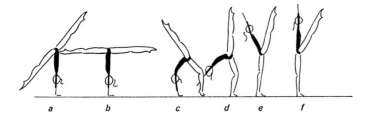

a   *b*   *c*   *d*   *e*   *f*

The head should be in a neutral position, with the eyes just able to see the hands. The head stays in this position until the hands leave the floor and then it is brought through so that the trailing leg can be seen as the body moves to the vertical.

As the second leg leaves the floor, the gymnast should be in balance on her hands, with the trunk of the body as long and as straight as possible as she passes through the vertical (b). She then extends the shoulders backwards and brings the leading foot to the floor as close to the hands as possible. This support leg will bend slightly to get the foot closer to the hands (c). The gymnast then moves the balance point from the hands to the foot and begins to stand up (d). The leading leg and hips will have to move slightly in front of the support leg to counterbalance the weight of the upper body (e). Eventually she will come to the finishing position, leaning back slightly to counterbalance the leg held up in front.

Mechanics of the move

As the gymnast lunges forwards to place her hands on the floor her CG is relatively low, and well behind her hands. By extending the forward leg the gymnast exerts a force on the ground, which simultaneously exerts a reaction force of equal magnitude on the gymnast. It is this reaction force that overcomes the retarding effect of gravity and causes the gymnast to rotate about her wrists.

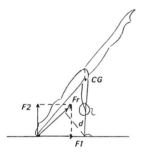

By pressing the shoulders backwards as she passes through the handstand split position, the gymnast keeps her CG over the hands for as long as possible and enables the leading foot to be placed as close as possible to the hands. Without this shoulder movement the gymnast's CG would fall outside her support base as the foot reaches for the ground. The further away from the base the weight acts, the greater the turning force acting on the gymnast, and the less controlled the movement will appear. Minimising the distance between her hands and the first foot also reduces the amount of force required to move the gymnast's CG onto this new base. She then uses muscular strength to lift the body to the vertical finishing position. The diagram that follows shows good shoulder, hip and back flexibility (a). The CG of the body only has to move a small distance to be over the support point. This will allow good control and require little push from the hands. As the body becomes less flexible the CG is further from the support, as shown in (b) and (c), so the gymnast has to push off the hands to get the CG slightly in front of the support leg to balance the trunk during the stand-up phase of the move.

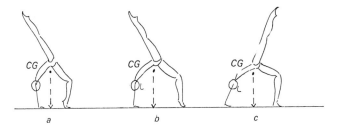

Progressions

Key points

- Flexibility in shoulders, hips and back.
- The leading foot must be placed close to the hands in the second phase of the move.

1. Get the gymnast to kick to handstand and whilst supporting her make her consciously move her shoulders backwards in preparation for the controlled placement of the leading foot on the floor.

2. Ask her to do the same practice again, but after moving the shoulders she should place both feet on the floor in front of her, with control.

3. Get the gymnast to repeat progression 2 and then to stand up. The knees may bend slightly to bring the feet closer to the hands.

4. The gymnast should now kick to a split handstand, concentrating on a straight back and maximum split of the legs.

5. She should repeat progression 4, and then press the shoulders through to place the leading foot on the floor.

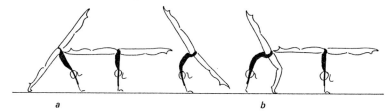

  Moving from (a) to (b) several times is useful to gain control and feel the balance necessary to complete the move.

6. The last phase of the move to be practised is standing up on the support leg and keeping the free leg as high as possible. The hands should be placed a specific distance from a set of wall bars and the gymnast should assume the position where the support leg is on the floor and the hands can then lift to the vertical. The second leg will stop when it touches the wall bars. The more supple the gymnast is, the closer she will be able to get to the wall bars.

Specific conditioning

1. Shoulder flexibility. Sit the gymnast by a set of wall bars, put a rolled-up mat behind her shoulders and ask her to reach back to hold a wall bar. This stretches the muscles around the shoulder girdle.

2. Put the gymnast in splits on a set of wall bars and get her to pull towards the bars with constant pressure to reach a 180° split. This should be done on both legs, not just the one that is dominant in the walkover.

3. Whilst in the position for (2), the body can also perform a strength exercise. The gymnast moves her shoulders towards the floor and then returns them to the leading knee. It is important that this exercise also is done on both legs.

4. The gymnast needs to have the strength to hold the leg as high as possible at the completion of the move. Whilst stabilising herself at a ballet barre, get her to lift, not swing, the leg as high as possible and hold for a second. Do this for ten repetitions and then hold the position for ten seconds. Both legs should be lifted forwards, to the side and backwards.

Backward walkover

The backward walkover is an aesthetically pleasing move provided that the gymnast has good flexibility. The hips and shoulders need to rotate through 180°, more if possible. The preparation for this move involves standing on one leg with the toes of the other foot just touching the floor for balance.

The back should be straight, the arms above the head but with the shoulders relaxed. The gymnast then lifts her leading leg as high as possible, extends through the shoulders and presses them back at the same time.

The gymnast now moves her hands backwards towards the floor, extending the legs through to an arc of 180° plus.

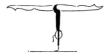

The closer the hands can be placed to the support foot, the smaller the adjustment the gymnast has to make to reach the new balance position, and the greater the control she will have.

From the split handstand position the gymnast brings her leading foot as close to the hands as possible, again minimising the adjustments required to reach the next balance position.

From this point the weight of the body is carefully transferred to the support leg whilst the hands leave the floor. Keeping the trunk as straight as possible, the gymnast should lift up to the vertical, ensuring that the trailing leg is kept as high and as extended as possible.

The gymnast should finish the walkover on one leg with the second leg held as high as possible behind her. The body should be straight and vertical, with the shoulders in a relaxed position.

Mechanics of the move

For the strong and very supple gymnast, the controlled backward arch of the body is accompanied by a slight forward movement of the hips, which keeps the CG above the support base (the gymnast's foot). As the hands are placed on the ground, the gymnast pushes with the support foot to move her CG over her hands.

She then uses muscular strength to tip her legs to the horizontal splits position.

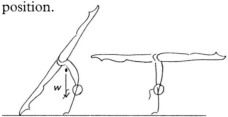

She must be able to place the leading foot close to the hands without losing balance, and then transfer her weight over this base and lift to the finishing position.

Unfortunately, such complete flexibility is not universal!

The less supple gymnast begins the walkover like her more flexible counterpart, leaning backwards under control. However, as she reaches the limits of her flexibility she is no longer able to keep her CG over her support base, and so the whole body begins to rotate about her supporting foot. The further from her body the gymnast's weight acts, the greater the turning force created and the less controlled the gymnast appears to be as she reaches for the floor. Since the gymnast's inflexibility prevents her from placing her hands near her foot, she must produce a greater thrust to move her CG over her hands to a position from which she can lift to the split handstand position.

Where inflexibility and/or lack of strength causes the lead foot to be placed far from the hands, the gymnast will again be off balance, this time rotating about her hands, and needing a strong thrust to move her CG over her foot.

Progressions

Key points

- Good flexibility in the shoulder joint, hip joint and back.
- The hands must be placed on the floor close to the supporting foot in the first phase of the move.
- The leading foot must be placed close to the hands in the second phase of the move.

1. Have the gymnast kick to handstand against a bar and practice splitting the legs for the second part of the walkover.

2. Using a box top or rolled up mat, get the gymnast to go to a bridge position and kick through the split handstand. The height of the box can change as the gymnast becomes more proficient.

3. The same skill as progression 2, but using the floor.

4. To practise keeping the leading leg as high as possible at the start, the gymnast can rest it on a ballet barre and walkover away from the barre.

Specific conditioning

This move does not need any particular strength exercises, so long as the gymnast can kick to handstand and support her weight in the bridge position. What is necessary is the ability to extend through the shoulders and the hips. There are many flexibility techniques available. With minimal supervision and the gymnast working unaided, the following exercises would be helpful.

1. Sit the gymnast in front of a set of wall bars with a rolled up mat behind her shoulders. She should stretch backwards and hold on to a wall bar, thus applying pressure to the shoulder girdle.

2. The gymnast must be able to sit in the splits position. If a gymnast cannot sit in splits, the weight of her body is sufficient to stretch the muscles around the hip girdle. If an arm is placed by the opposite knee (i.e. right arm by left knee), this will help to keep the body in alignment.

3. Using wall bars, get the gymnast to lift her leading leg as high as possible and pull the body towards the bars. Alignment of the body is very important. More supple gymnasts can take down the shoulders towards the floor whilst still holding on to the wall bars.

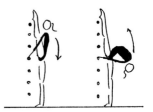

Cartwheel

This move can be done slowly or with speed. It can be a move in its own right or an accelerator into another move. It is a very versatile element and can be taught in many ways. It can start sideways or forwards; it can finish sideways or with a quarter turn in. The most useful technique is a forward-facing entry to finish with a quarter turn in.

It is possible to start the move with both feet together, with the left foot in front of the right or vice versa, with one leg lifted before or after moving and so on. These are all variations on a theme. The smaller the number of variables, the easier and more successful the teaching will be. To cut down on such variables, the gymnast should start with both feet together. She leans forwards until she is off balance, and then takes a long step forward. In this starting position the arms should be above the

Natalia Ilienko, USSR

head and parallel. Initially the shoulders should be relaxed; then they extend as the hands make contact with the floor. If a gymnast lunges forwards with her left foot leading, then, just before the left hand reaches the floor, the right shoulder should be pulled back through 90°. This helps to maintain a good line through the body and does not allow the arms to cross in front of the face. The leading hand should be placed a reasonable distance from the leading leg. This helps to keep the leading leg directed through the vertical plane and to prevent the legs from going 'around the side', causing an imbalance on landing.

When the gymnast is on her hands, her body should be straight, with the legs fully stretched.

As the first leg is about to land, the hips should turn through 90° so that the body will finish facing the direction it came from. The arms lift off the floor, and if the cartwheel is to be followed by a back handspring the second leg should be placed by the side of the first. If the cartwheel is to be performed on the beam, the second leg should be placed in line with, but behind, the first leg. In this case the first leg would need to bend slightly. The arms should stay above the head and parallel to each other throughout the move. The head should stay in a neutral plane to help keep the back straight.

Mechanics of the move

From standing, the gymnast will use the skeletal muscles to move her CG in front of her feet. Rotation will then occur about the feet due to the turning force created by the weight of the body acting outside the support base (that is, the force is eccentric).

Once the gymnast has lunged forwards and placed her hands on the floor, she must move her CG up and over this new base. She achieves this by thrusting downwards and backwards with her second leg. The resultant reaction force (Fr) exerted by the floor on the gymnast produces the required movement, overcoming the retarding effect of gravity.

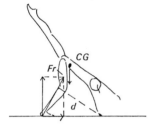

In the second half of the cartwheel, as the gymnast moves from hands to feet, her weight (W) again acts outside her support base (the hands). In this phase the effect of gravity is to enhance the rotation about the hands.

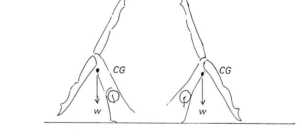

The gymnast makes a 90° turn by using the muscles of the body.

Progressions

Key points

- The move must go through a vertical plane.
- Good shoulder alignment, showing a neutral head position.
- A good 'box' splits in handstand.

1. A handstand.

2. Whilst in a supported handstand, the gymnast moves from side to side so that each hand takes the body weight independently. Each hand only needs to leave the floor by about 5–10 cm.

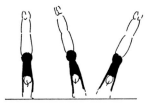

3. Ask the gymnast to do the first half of the cartwheel, until she is in a handstand with her legs in splits. Stop her at this point: it is a 'memory' position.

4. Once this has been done, the second half can be added to the first. Again, support should be given so that the gymnast can feel the correct positions and the muscle groups that are to be used.

5. Once the whole move has been taught, a smooth wall can be used so that the gymnast can check that she is moving through the vertical plane. She can do cartwheels with the face towards the wall and away from the wall.

Specific conditioning

If a good handstand can be held then strength of support is not needed. It is good flexibility that is necessary.

If the cartwheel is to be performed with maximum amplitude the gymnast must pay attention to the box splits position. The best way to prepare this shape is to slide down between two low beams, keeping the body straight and allowing gravity to do the work. Holding this position for 20–30 seconds will help to stretch the muscles around the hip girdle, and many repetitions will help the gymnast to learn the shape.

Forward handspring

The handspring is a move that can be used either as an element by itself or as an accelerator into another move. The techniques of the two versions are very similar, the major difference being the angle at which the body strikes the floor.

Entry (a) shows a very fast rotation but little flight. Entry (b) shows that great height has been achieved, but little rotation has been generated.

To start the move it helps to have some forward speed, say three or four running steps, before the hurdle step. The body should be leaning forwards at about 45° with the arms over the head and with no shoulder angle (a).

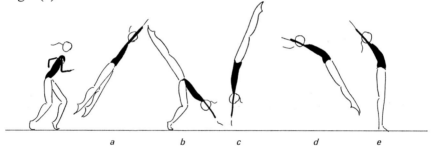

Assuming the gymnast wishes to use the handspring as an accelerator, when the feet make contact with the floor she should place her hands on the floor close to her leading foot (b). The arms stay by the head and the shoulder angle should stay open. Unless the gymnast is extremely strong, a closed shoulder angle is likely to collapse slightly on impact, increasing the time spent in contact with the floor, rather than achieving the rapid rebound that is required.

The first leg drives as hard as it can, causing the gymnast to rotate about her wrists. The first leg should be stopped and 'caught up' by the second. The shoulders extend when the hands are in contact with the floor (b–c) to aid height and rotation.

When the gymnast makes contact with the floor again she should do so in an arched position just short of the vertical (e). This position is ideal since the muscles down the front of the body are on 'stretch' ready for a fast contraction into the next forward move.

Mechanics of the move

Each leg in turn drives off the floor with vertical and horizontal forces
F1 and F2 respectively. The resultant force (Fr) causes rotation about
the wrists.

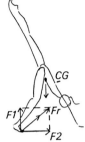

The diagram below shows the point of release from the floor and the
forces which are acting on the body. Just prior to this point the gymnast
makes a shoulder extension which results in vertical and horizontal
reaction forces (F1 and F2 respectively). The resultant force (Fr) does
not pass through the CG point and therefore rotation and height are
affected.

Progressions

Key points

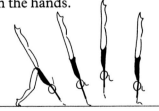

- Strong leg thrust.
- Good shoulder alignment.
- Strong repulsion off the hands.

1. The gymnast should kick to handstand.
2. Again, she should kick to handstand vigorously, fixing the feet in
    line with the rest of the body, and hop on the hands.

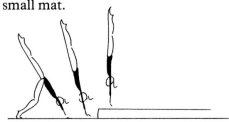

3. This is the same practice as progression (2) but the gymnast should
    now land on a small mat.

4. Have the gymnast work down an inclined platform with a handspot from the coach on the upper arm and lower back.

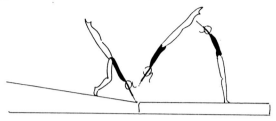

5. A flat approach can now be used. It is helpful to use a muscle replacement in the form of a trampette with a mat covering the whole working surface. Once the gymnast has been shaped correctly in (4), she should be able to do this practice keeping good body form.

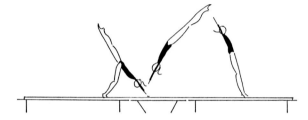

6. Now take away the muscle replacement, but still give the gymnast a little more air time than normal by using a two-mat platform.

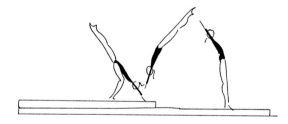

7. A very soft sprung tumble run could be an advantage when attempting the whole move.

Specific conditioning

The same muscle actions are needed in this move as are used for the handspring vault, so the conditioning exercises are the same (see pp. 99–101).

Round-off

Many moves in gymnastics are known by more than one name. The round-off is also known as an arab spring. The back handspring is also known as a back flip or flic-flac, and in North America it is known as the flip-flop.

The technique described here may not suit all gymnasts. The arm action coming out of the round-off and the back handspring is a dropped arm action. It is very effective but it is probably best suited to the gymnast with fast muscle twitch fibres. If gymnasts with a lower percentage of fast muscle twitch fibres wish to perform these elements effectively, they may need to move the arms towards the head earlier in anticipation of the next move. It must always be remembered that gymnasts are individuals and should be treated as such. Every technique must be adapted for the individual. The elements described below are no different.

The round-off is rated the second most important move after the handstand. It is now performed on all four pieces of apparatus. If taught correctly in the first place, the muscle education should carry across to different apparatus quite easily.

The aim of the round-off is to maintain forward velocity whilst turning through 180°.

In recent years floor surfaces have become faster, as they have progressed from coconut matting through rubber and foam mats to modern surfaces laid onto airballs and rubber and steel springs. This means gymnasts must become faster too. The coach must accept this and adjust techniques accordingly. The round-off should finish in a position which will allow the gymnast to take off for a back handspring.

After a few strides the gymnast should gather her arms for the hurdle step. The arms must swing from the hips to a point above the head (a), but the shoulder angle must be open when the gymnast makes contact with the floor (d).

a   b   c   d   e   f   g

On landing from the hurdle step (b), both legs should initially bend and then straighten forcefully as the gymnast reaches into the round-off. If the gymnast performs the approach and round-off on a line, the feet should land on this line from the hurdle step.

The gymnast should stay facing forward for as long as possible, maintaining forward velocity (c). Only at the last moment should she

Svetlana Baitova, USSR

torque twist the body to create the turn (d), placing her hands on either side of the line described above.

There has been great controversy about exactly where to place the hands – on the line, or across it. Physiologically, the pressure sustained by the second wrist can be reduced if this hand is placed near, but not on, the line.

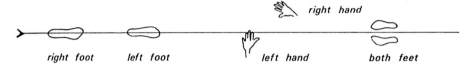

right hand

right foot   left foot   left hand   both feet

With the shoulder angle open and the muscles down the front of the body fully stretched, the gymnast is ready to 'snap' the feet to the floor whilst at the same time 'snapping' the chest to the ceiling (e) and (f). The movement of both parts of the body rotating together should mean the gymnast finishes with the feet making contact with the floor and the shoulders behind the feet (g). It is possible to keep the body in a straight line, and so when the feet make contact with the floor they should punch into it the same way as they would for a salto; the gymnast should not land, sink and then push off. The reaction of modern floor areas is now fast enough to accept this technique.

Mechanics of the move

After the run and hurdle step the gymnast places one hand on the floor and pivots about that fixed point until the other hand reaches the floor. The twist about the long axis is achieved by applying a torque to the floor. At the same time both legs independently drive from the floor to create rotation. The first leg creates rotation about the second leg (a) and this in turn creates rotation about the hands (b).

When the gymnast is on her hands (c) the horizontal and vertical ground reaction forces will have a resultant force behind the CG and will therefore create rotation. Additional forces are created by a short

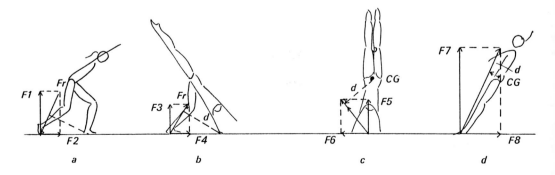

a   b   c   d

powerful contraction of the muscles down the front of the body to aid rotation from the hands.

At point (d) there is a resultant ground reaction force in front of the gymnast's CG, so rotation is created for the back handspring. An additional force will be exerted into the floor by the arms driving quickly above the head in preparation for the back handspring. The ground reaction force to this action will help rotation of the back handspring.

Progressions

Key points

- Strong leg drive onto the hands.
- Fully open shoulder angle when the hands make contact with the floor.
- An off-balance finishing position with the shoulders well behind the feet.

1. The gymnast should perform a handstand with full shoulder extension.

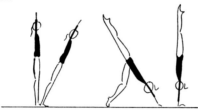

2. Then cartwheel one quarter turn in, to finish off-balance. Initially to be done slowly, but then with more speed.

3. Progression 2 can now be attempted from the end of a bench or platform, onto a safety landing module.

4. Using the same set-up as in (3), the gymnast should join the legs more rapidly and try to get some repulsion from the shoulders.

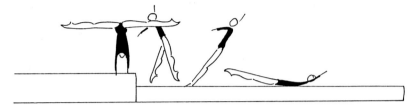

5. To create more repulsion from the arms a 'muscle replacer' (e.g. a trampette) can be used. The gymnast must close her legs before they reach the landing module. At this point it cannot be stressed enough that the landing surface must be of sufficiently high quality to ensure that the skill can be practised safely.

6. Once the gymnast can land on her feet and then fall onto her back, the whole move can be made more aggressive by asking the gymnast to join the feet as early as possible in the air and land on her back without her feet touching at all. Initially a coach should support the gymnast to make sure that she does not over-rotate.

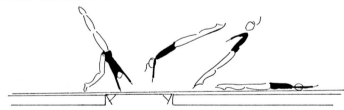

7. More repulsion from the hands is now required and the legs should join before they reach the safety landing module.

8. To increase awareness and emphasis of the strong leg drive and rapid 'snap' of the body, the gymnast should now be asked to rotate onto her back. Again the coach should initially stand in to cope with any unforeseen eventualities.

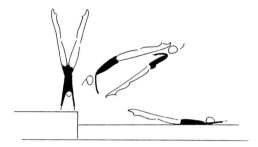

9. The whole move can now be taken back to the floor. Different levels of mats can be used to aid the flight from the hands. Care should be taken to protect the gymnast when she lands in the desired position. A round-off is an accelerator and the gymnast should be off-balance when she lands. Therefore, whenever progressions for the move are performed some method of bringing the gymnast to a safe standstill is required.

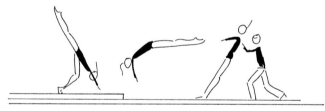

Specific conditioning

1. Leg conditioning should be of the plyometric type (i.e. rebound work). This should only be done with well-conditioned gymnasts, and even then only for short periods. Pre-pubescent gymnasts can develop achilles tendon strain if they are worked too hard. In the exercise shown here, the gymnast should rebound between the two springboards.

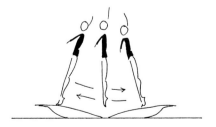

2. Shoulder conditioning should be done with speed.

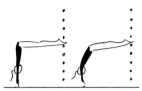

3. With the gymnast's shoulders and feet on low supports, ask her to move the body from a convex to a concave body shape and vice-versa.

4. The gymnast should kick to handstand on a support platform and 'snap', or rapidly contract the muscles down the front of the body. This is a very powerful action which conditions the muscles so that they can rotate the body.

Back handspring

The shape of the back handspring has changed over the years and some shapes have been more effective than others. A gymnast may select a technique to suit her own strength, speed or power. If she finished the round-off as described in the previous section, she would be in a perfect position to stay straight and rotate the back handspring as fast as possible at a height at which the hands just touch the floor. Most female gymnasts do not have powerfully developed upper bodies, so this technique would suit them. When the gymnast's hands make contact with the floor there should be a very slight arch down the length of the body to facilitate the 'snap' action as described in the round-off. The result of this action is to increase angular momentum in the post-flight.

The advantage of this technique is that the gymnast rotates very quickly about her hands and also from her hands to her feet. Consequently she applies a large force to the floor as she lands. This force can then be

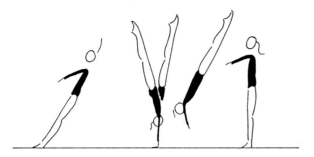

used for complex saltos, as long as the body is in maximum tension when it makes contact with the floor. Slower gymnasts tend to adapt this technique to suit their body type.

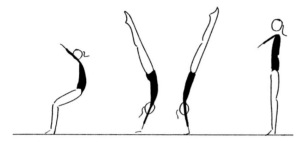

Whichever back handspring technique is used, the head should stay in a neutral position throughout the move.

Mechanics of the move

The end of the round-off is the beginning of the back handspring. As the feet make contact with the ground from the round-off, the gymnast exerts a force forwards and downwards. The ground reaction force is in the opposite directions, upwards (F1) and backwards (F2). The resultant force Fr is eccentric and therefore causes rotation. Additional rotational forces can be applied by gymnasts if the arm action out of the round-off into the back handspring is delayed.

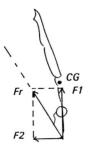

When the gymnast lands on her hands she exerts a downward and backward force on the ground. The resultant reaction force (Fr) is eccentric and therefore rotation occurs.

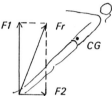

Whilst the gymnast is in contact with the floor she applies an additional force to it by contracting the muscles down the front of the body. This 'snap' action causes the gymnast to rotate very quickly to her feet.

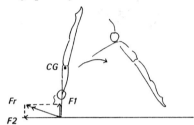

Progressions

Key points

- Rotate about the hands very quickly.
- Shoulder and hip angles must be open when the hands make contact with the floor.
- Shoulders must rotate *from* the floor as quickly as the feet rotate *to* the floor.

Obviously, a human being only has eyes on one side of the body! A gymnast will travel quite happily in the direction she can see, but will often be more cautious about travelling backwards. When a back handspring is to be taught, the gymnast is likely to be apprehensive. Care must be taken to develop her spatial and kinaesthetic awareness so as to alleviate some of this anxiety.

1. Have the gymnast stand upright with her arms straight and by her ears. The hands should be very slightly turned in so that when they make contact with the floor the elbow can flex very slightly to absorb the impact.

    Now have two supporters lean the gymnast so that they can feel the off-balance starting position and then very slowly lift the gymnast and rotate her backwards onto her hands. Make sure that there is no change in body shape. The gymnast should step out of this position, not come down with both feet together. If this happens the gymnast may educate the wrong muscle groups for the second part of the back handspring.

    To lessen the gymnast's anxiety, this work should be done on a safety landing module.

2. Using a trampette and safety landing modules, the same exercise can be done with a small bounce. Finally it can be done with the dropped arm action. Support by the coach should be given at all stages for some time, until the move has been well learned.

3. The 'snap' action from the handstand needs to be taught carefully. The gymnast may need shaping for this action. Many gymnasts only use their hip flexors, which reduces the effectiveness of the move, instead of using all the muscles down the front of the body.

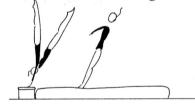

4. The trampoline is an ideal 'muscle replacer' for gymnasts attempting a back handspring. As soon as the body shaping and muscle education has been done (progression 3), the move can be attempted on the trampoline. Trampolines situated in a pit are ideal. If regular trampolines are used then safety modules and spotters should be in place in case the gymnast travels too far.

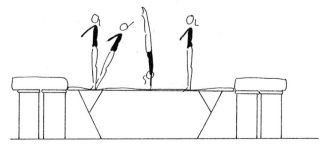

5. The gymnast should now be ready to attempt the whole move on a regular tumbling surface with support. Eventually the back handspring should be linked with a cartwheel as shown below (a), and then a round-off (b).

6. If a tumble track is available then the gymnast should be encouraged to do rebound saltos. The gymnast should try to keep her body straight throughout and the arm action should be the same as that used in the back handspring. The diagram below shows the landing and take-off positions of the saltos.

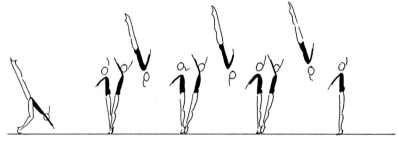

Specific conditioning

1. The same exercises apply as those given for the round-off (pp. 185–186).
2. The arms should not take a great deal of pressure using the correct technique, so a general conditioning programme should suffice. Should the gymnast miscalculate and have to take heavy pressure on the arms, some fast handstand press-ups with support may be useful to give her added strength.

3. Conditioning for the trunk is very important. During the move the body changes shape from a slightly convex to a slightly concave shape. This exercise should be done slowly at first to get the shape and muscle education correct. It can then be performed more quickly.

Tuck back salto

When starting on backward saltos, most coaches teach the tuck position first. Theoretically it is the most difficult of the simple saltos, in terms of the number of angles which have to be put in the body and the consequent number of variables. The pike back has one angle and the straight back has none. The arm actions for the three versions – straight, piked and tucked – are virtually identical. The advantage that the tuck back version offers is that the tuck shape is easier to rotate, and so it is more suitable for the beginner gymnast.

The tuck back salto can be done from stand or from an accelerator such as a round-off or back handspring. The most common entry is from a back handspring, so it is worth explaining this technique.

When the gymnast lands from her back handspring she should be in a slightly dished, very tight shape. Tension throughout the body is necessary if the forces created at impact are to have maximum effect. Many gymnasts land with an arch in the lower back and the chest leaning forwards, which is detrimental to good rotation. The arms should be above and slightly in front on the head, which should be in a neutral position throughout the move. The angle at which the gymnast lands from the back handspring and takes off into the salto will depend upon the speed of the back handspring and the characteristics of the tumbling surface. The more rotation the gymnast generates in the back handspring, the smaller the angle of strike can be. The faster the floor surface, the greater the angle of strike can be. The following diagram shows the different flight paths of the CG of the gymnast resulting from different angles of take-off.

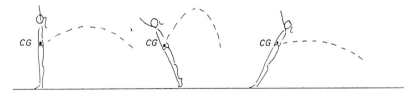

Just before take-off, the hips should be driven forwards and upwards, and the body should adopt a slightly arched shape. When the gymnast has left the floor, she tucks by bringing the knees to the chest as the arms move down to grasp the knees. The back should stay straight throughout. When the gymnast can see the floor she should extend the body in preparation for landing, taking the arms sideways and forwards to improve stability.

When the hands go to the knees for the tuck position, it is possible to take hold of the front or the back of the knees. It is more efficient for the gymnast to hold the front of the knees because she can compress the body closer to the line of rotation. If the gymnast were to go on to do triple back saltos, then she would have no option but to take the front of the knees, and so she may as well just learn one technique and start with her hands in front.

To land the salto correctly, with no over-rotation and large steps, the gymnast must consciously open her hip angle at some point in the salto to get the body back in line and ready to take the impact. If she doesn't, when the feet make contact with the ground the hips will be behind the feet and over-rotation will occur.

Mechanics of the move

It makes no difference whether the move is preceded by an accelerator or not; the principles of the mechanics are still the same, although the magnitude and direction of the forces will change.

At the point of take-off the gymnast extends her legs into the floor, exerting a downward forward force on the ground. The resultant ground reaction force acts eccentrically (i.e. not through the CG), producing rotation. The magnitude of this force can be increased by (1) increasing the rotation in the back handspring, and (2) by lifting the arms rapidly during contact with the ground.

Once the gymnast is airborne she cannot alter her flight path, nor can she vary her angular momentum. However, by changing her shape she can alter the rate at which she rotates. When she tucks, and brings her mass closer to the axis of rotation, she increases the rate at which she rotates. When she extends for the landing, she increases her body length, extending the 'lever' and decreasing the speed of rotation.

Progressions

Key points

- Take off with good body tension.
- Take off from the floor with the body stretched and hips elevated.
- After take-off, quickly bring the mass of the body as close to the axis of rotation as possible.

1. Coach and gymnast bounce together on a trampoline, then the gymnast takes off and rotates to the horizontal, the coach stays on the bed of the trampoline and supports her in this position momentarily.

2. The gymnast performs the same actions as in progression 1. On the coach's signal, the gymnast should tuck her knees to her chest. The coach must be prepared for additional rotation and make sure that the gymnast does not complete the salto.

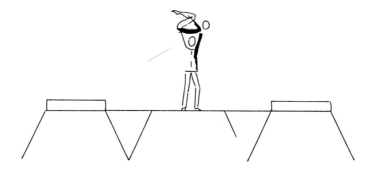

3. The gymnast can now do the same progression as (2), and complete the salto. If she has not enough rotation, the coach can add a little more force with the hand which is on her lower back to improve the rotation.

When the coach releases the hand on the upper body (b) he then moves to a position where he can support the gymnast's front and back to stabilise the landing (c).

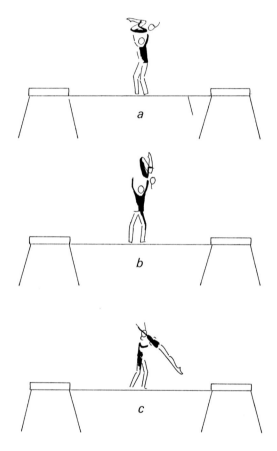

If coaches are not confident to hand support at stages (b) and (c), it is quite acceptable to use an overhead spotting rig. A little of the control may be lost, but safety is always the biggest concern. The gymnast will eventually have to come out of the spotting rig and a hand spot will be necessary. To give the gymnast a little more confidence when she is attempting the move by herself for the first time, the coach may throw a safety landing module on the bed after she has taken off and before she has landed.

If a trampoline is not available then it is possible to do the same progressions from a trampette.

4. The gymnast should be allowed to practise joining the back handspring to the salto.

   A handstand on a soft mat stack 70 cm high, followed by a 'snap down' of the legs and a 'snap up' of the chest to rebound from the floor and land on the mat with straight legs, would be desirable.

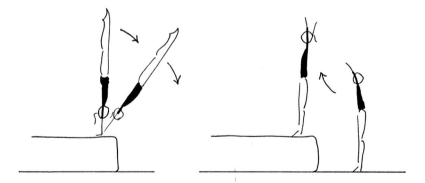

5. After rebounding to the soft mat with straight legs, the gymnast is ready to add more rotation and land on her back on the mat. A very strong arm action and hip extension will be needed to achieve this progression. In the initial stages of learning this practice, some gymnasts rotate but do not travel far enough forwards to land on

the mat on their back. A coach should stand in until they are familiar with the practice.

6. The gymnast should now be ready to do progressions (1), (2) and (3) from a standing back handspring, and then add a round-off and finally some steps.

Specific conditioning

1. Plyometric training (rebound) is useful. Care should be taken with young gymnasts not to do too much. Osgood-Schlatters Disease and Severs Disease can result if the training is too hard too soon.

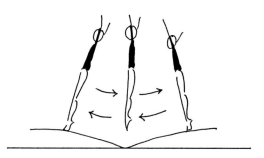

Rebound jumping from two springboards

2. Landing from different heights forwards and backwards. The salto landing itself can be used to strengthen the exact muscles which are going to be used. This should only be incorporated into the conditioning programme once the skill has been learned.

Full twisting back salto

A salto with full twist is now being performed on all pieces of apparatus and so it becomes an important element. There is a strong overlap between each version, so if body shape and muscle education are taught correctly, the teaching of this element on each piece of apparatus will be easier and less time-consuming.

It is important to decide which technique to use. The element can be taught using a half turn into a front salto, and then a front salto with a half turn out (Arabian in and a barani out). It can also be taught using a straight salto backwards with a 360° twist. Both techniques are acceptable and look exactly the same, but the performer's concept of how and when to twist is totally different.

The majority of female gymnasts are taught to perform this element with the concept of a straight salto and add a 360° twist. To do this the gymnast must have a good take-off position at the end of the round-off or back handspring. In this take-off or 'set' position, the arms should be above the head and the shoulders above the feet, so that the gymnast's CG will be on or just in front of the vertical line. On take-off the hips will thrust forwards and upwards.

The twist can be initiated by the tilt or torque technique. Both are valid and work equally well, but most gymnasts use the torque technique.

Just before take-off the gymnast turns her hips and shoulders slightly to one side to create a torque effect. This effect can be increased or decreased by the width setting of the arms. Initially when gymnasts learn this element they tend to set their arms very wide, but when their muscles have learned what to do they become more efficient and the width of the arms can be reduced. At a later stage, when double or triple twists are taught, the arms are set wide again.

As soon as the gymnast is airborne she must bring the arms into the body to conserve rotation and accelerate the twist. The exact placement of the arms is not important, but they should be as close to the line of twist as possible. It is a good idea to bring the forearms down the line of the chest, keeping the elbows as close together as possible.

If the gymnast is very efficient in the twist then it will be finished by the time the body has reached the vertical. The rest of the time in the air can be spent preparing for the landing.

Throughout the move, the head should be kept in a neutral position so that when the upper body turns, the head will turn with it.

When the gymnast leaves the floor she must have in mind the concept of twisting 'down', that is, twisting with the head pointing at the floor.

When she lands, the gymnast should have her feet shoulder width apart, the calf and thigh muscles taking most of the strain and keeping the back straight.

Oksana Omeliantchik, USSR

Mechanics of the move

On take-off from the floor there are two ground reaction forces (F1 and F2) resulting in one force (Fr) a distance (d) from the CG of the body. This creates an eccentric force (i.e. not going through the CG) and therefore creates rotation about the transverse axis.

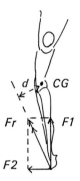

At the same time the body creates a torque twist. If the twist is to the left, the left shoulder is pulled back, and vice-versa. If necessary, this technique can also be coupled with a tilt twist technique. On take-off the gymnast not only pulls the left shoulder back but also drops the left arm towards the left hip (a). This causes an action/reaction and the body tilts to the right (b). The salto is now tilted and therefore twists. Before landing, the arm actions must be reversed to correct the tilt (c).

To conserve rotation about the transverse and longitudinal axis, the arms are brought in to the body as close to the CG as possible. A rounding of the shoulders and the forearms down the line of the chest is desirable (b).

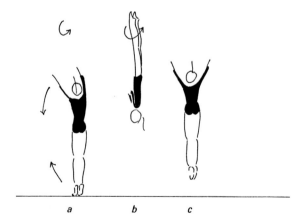

Take-off as viewed from the rear

Progressions

Key points

- On take-off, think of height and rotation first and twist second.
- Twist with the body in a straight line.
- Twist with the eyes always spotting the floor.

It is desirable to use a muscle replacer at this early stage so that a high number of repetitions can take place and the gymnast can concentrate on learning the skill rather than worrying about landing and early fatigue. When gymnasts experience anxiety or fear about a move or part of it, they stop learning. It is better to make the learning situation as simple as possible. The progressions for this move are all done using a bench leading up to a trampette. When the element has been taught correctly here, it can be taken to a sprung tumbling surface and then to a regular competition floor.

1. The gymnast should do a straight back salto. Emphasis should be on the arms lifting above the head on take-off (a) and then being brought down sharply to touch the front of the thigh when she can see the landing surface (b). Just prior to landing the arms should be taken forward and sideways from the body to give stability to the landing and eventually to stop the twist that will have been initiated.

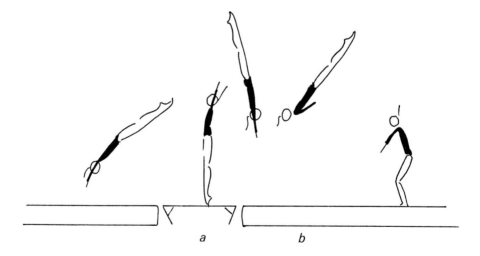

a   b

2. The gymnast performs the same salto, but at the point where she brought her arms down to her thighs she now brings them down and across the body, keeping them parallel. This arm action makes the body tilt, and causes twist. The head will move with the shoulders.

It is useful to get the gymnast to perform this body action before it is put into the salto. There should be no wriggle, nor should one half of the body turn before the rest. If this happens, the gymnast has not initiated a tilt twist.

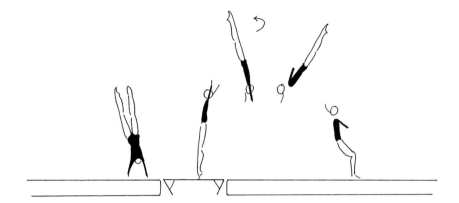

3.   The arm action for the next progression also needs to be practised first in isolation and then put into the salto. The timing of when to move the arms is still the same, but their movement is different. The gymnast should be told to lower the arms in the same direction as before, but when they get to her shoulder height she must bring them into her body as quickly as possible. This action should create the full twist.

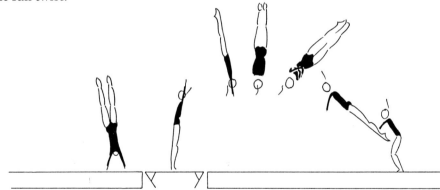

It must be remembered that these progressions will teach the timing of this twist in the latter stages of the salto. When the move is being performed to its maximum, the 360° of twist will have been completed by the time the gymnast has completed 180° of rotation of the salto. With time, orientation and efficiency, the gymnast should naturally accommodate an earlier twist until it eventually becomes a torque twist.

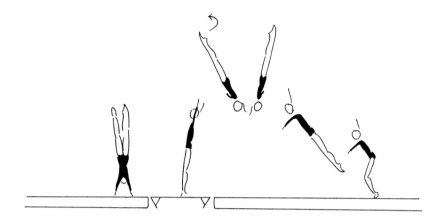

It is sometimes useful to handspot the gymnast through the move to show her the timing of the twist in relation to the salto.

Spotting a left twist

Now that the twist has been learnt it needs to be taken to the competition floor. Initially a sprung tumble run should be used, with a soft landing area for the salto. The gymnast is asked to do a round-off back handspring half twisting salto. Many gymnasts will automatically do the full twist because of the work already covered on the trampette. It is useful to insist on the half twist, not only because it can be used as an element in its own right, but because if the full twist is going wrong at a later time the gymnast can be asked to go back a progression and retrieve the situation.

When the full twist has been successfully completed the move can be performed to land on the tumble strip.

When the gymnast becomes familiar with this she can transfer it to a regular floor area.

If more twists are required, they should also be added in half twists for the same reasons, and again started on the trampette.

Specific conditioning

1. The same conditioning is needed for a salto with a twist as without. This work has already been covered (see pp. 196–197).
2. The new part of the element is the torque for the twist. Have the gymnast lie down with her thighs across a box and with the legs fixed. Get her to do back lifts to the horizontal with an alternate twist to left and right each time. After the gymnast has learned the exercise the lift with twist section can be done at speed as it will be in the move. Care must be taken not to twist and stop so fast that a muscle may be 'pulled'.

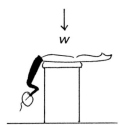  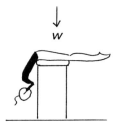

Bibliography

Australian Coaching Council, (1980), *Towards Better Coaching*. Canberra, Australian Government Publishing Service.

Canadian Gymnastic Federation, (1984), *Coaching Certification Program*, Ontario, Canadian Gymnastic Federation.

Encyclopaedia of Sports Medicine 1, (1988), Oxford, Blackwell Scientific Publications.

Fédération Internationale Gymnastique (FIG), (1989 edition), *Code of Points*, Switzerland.

Grayson, Edward, *Sport and the Law*, Sunday Telegraph Publication.

Hay, James G., (1985), *The Biomechanics of Sports Techniques*, Englewood Cliffs NJ, Prentice-Hall International Editions.

Klaffs, Carl and Arnheim, Daniel, (1977), *Modern Principles of Athletic Training*, St Louis, Mo, the C. V. Mosby Co.

Lamb, David R., (1984), *Physiology of Exercise*, London, Collier Macmillan.

National Coaching Foundation, (1984), Introductory Study Packs: *Mind over Matter* and *The Body in Action*.

Pasek, Vicki, (1990), 'Performers' rights in sport: where does copyright stand?', *Copyright World*, 8, Jan.–Feb. 1990.

Peterson, Lois and Renstrom, Per, (1988), *Sports Injuries*, London, Martin Dunitz.

Radcliffe, J. C. and Farentinos, R. C., (1985), *Plyometrics*. Champaign, Ill., Human Kinetics Publishers.

Sharkey, B. T., (1984), *Physiology of Fitness*. Champaign, Ill., Human Kinetics Publishers.

Schmidtbleicher, D., (1985), 'Strength training Part I: Classification of methods' and 'Strength training Part II: Structural analysis of motor strength qualities and its application to training', *Sports Science* (periodical on research and technology in sport, Aug. and Sept. 1985).

Wirhed, Rolf, (1984), *Athletic Ability and the Anatomy of Motion*, London, Wolfe Medical Publications.

Natalia Lashonova, USSR